HISTORIC TALES

of

Henry Cowell

REDWOODS STATE PARK

HISTORIC TALES
of
Henry Cowell
REDWOODS STATE PARK

BIG TREES GROVE

DEBORAH OSTERBERG

Foreword by William Tweed, author of *King Sequoia*

THE
History
PRESS

Published by The History Press
Charleston, SC
www.historypress.com

Front cover, top, left to right: Big Trees Grove was famous for its "sequestered by-paths…occupied by newly-married people, spooney couples and flirting pairs." *Author's personal collection*; Photographer William Sherer took this picture of his wife, Lulu, next to the Calling Card Tree at Cowell's Big Trees. *Santa Cruz Public Libraries, courtesy of Cynthia Mathews*; In the early 1880s, the Jumbo Tree was named for its resemblance to P.T. Barnum's famed circus elephant. *Author's personal collection*.

Back cover, top: John Charles Frémont and his family pose at the Fremont Tree on May 4, 1888. *Courtesy of Frank Perry*; *inset*: Poster of the Mary Pickford movie *A Romance of the Redwoods*, which was filmed at Big Trees Grove in 1917. *Wikimedia Commons*.

First published 2020

Manufactured in the United States

ISBN 9781467142953

Library of Congress Control Number: 2019954251

Notice: The information in this book is true and complete to the best of our knowledge. It is offered without guarantee on the part of the author or The History Press. The author and The History Press disclaim all liability in connection with the use of this book.

For my father and my brother
William "Bud" Osterberg and William "Big Bill" Osterberg Jr.

CONTENTS

Contents

FOREWORD

In the twenty-first century, California is blessed with an exceptional wealth of protected natural sites. Each year, tens of millions of Californians seek out these local, state and national parks with the hope of enjoying the Golden State's surpassing natural beauty and at the same time perhaps learning a bit more about themselves.

Surprisingly, even as we seek out these special places, we often know little about how they came to be. Instead, we all too often simply take our parks and other protected landscapes for granted. If we consider the question at all, it often comes down to no more than "how could our predecessors not have wanted to save this!"

The real stories, of course, are far more perilous. For every protected landscape in California, countless other priceless natural features disappeared to logging, agriculture or urban sprawl. For every protected stand of famous trees, uncounted acres of forests fell to the axe. The difference, almost always, can be found in a few key individuals who decided to make a difference despite the social currents of their times.

This book tells such a story. The story circles around the members of one particular family and how, despite the lack of useful financial or societal models, they kept the trees on their land standing through a time when those on neighboring tracts fell. Like all human stories, this one encompasses a full spectrum of human activity. We find not only vision but also greed, folly and short-sightedness.

FOREWORD

In documenting the story of the Welch family and the place they called "Big Trees Grove," author Deborah Osterberg captures a story that is both intimate and universal. We learn of a forest so famous that presidents came to visit and yet so precariously protected that the threat of complete destruction for financial gain continued to cast its dark shadow for almost two-thirds of a century.

As she pieces together this largely forgotten story, Osterberg makes an important contribution to the local history of the Santa Cruz Mountains while at the same time reminding Californians of their enduring relationship with all the state's many special places—a story that stretches from the pioneer days of the nineteenth century to the present.

The saga of this one small yet spectacular redwood grove also shares another important message—that the task of sustaining the Golden State's natural heritage is a responsibility that falls anew on each generation. In the human story of the Big Trees Grove at Henry Cowell Redwoods State Park, Osterberg reminds us that to explore our history is to come face to face with our own responsibilities.

—William Tweed

William Tweed is the author of *King Sequoia: The Tree that Inspired a Nation, Created Our National Park System, and Changed the Way We Think about Nature.*

PREFACE

As a new volunteer docent at Henry Cowell Redwoods State Park in 2016, I was asked an important question by park staff: what would be my interpretive focus? My answer—I wanted to bring the grove's historic postcards to life. After all, I'd been a historical reenactor and had everything I needed to dress as a Victorian visitor. In our docent class, we learned that in 1867, this grove of coast redwoods became the first to be preserved and open to the public, eventually becoming a resort known as Big Trees Grove. When I commenced my research in the small park library, I was disappointed to find very little information on the resort or its early tourists. Throughout the nineteenth century, the grove attracted thousands of visitors and dignitaries, yet there was no single book that told this engaging history.

Over the three years I conducted living history interpretation on the Redwood Loop Trail, I also compiled hundreds of newspaper articles and images of the grove's tourist history. It finally dawned on me that I could fill a gap in the written works on the park by transforming my research into a book. My goal was to let the resort's early visitors and proprietors tell their own stories in their own words. How was Big Trees Grove preserved? What attracted visitors to the grove? What modes of transportation and routes did they take to get here? What did visitors encounter upon arrival, and what were their impressions of the grove? Who were the proprietors of the resort, and what changes did they make to it? Did famous people visit the grove? And finally, what role did Big Trees Grove play in the preservation movement and the creation of redwood parks, particularly Big Basin?

My book provides a vivid portrait of the people who promoted, enjoyed and preserved this unique locale. I retraced this special story by using newspaper accounts, articles, visitor narratives, tourist guides, advertisements, postcards and rarely seen photographs. Of value to my research was the nineteenth-century custom of California traveling accounts being published in hometown newspapers across the country. Though I was not able to locate as much information as I wished about some of the early proprietors, my research did bring to light new and more detailed accounts of the tourist experience. Through extensive documentation, I was able to both dispel some myths as well as confirm some long-told stories. I include information on redwood ecology as appropriate and decided to limit reference to historical tree measurements since they are often unreliable.

Like many locals, I have visited the park since I was a child and excitedly recall the adventure of first entering the hollow base of the Fremont Tree. My family has deep redwood roots. The family affinity for redwoods began with my grandmother Ellen Osterberg Herman Hill, a member of the Santa Cruz Art League, who was known locally for her paintings of the Bonny Doon redwoods. My brother, "Big Bill" Osterberg, worked for the California State Parks for nearly thirty years and lived at Henry Cowell. So the park was literally my brother's backyard. Bill was the heavy equipment operator for the Santa Cruz District, and evidence of his many years of work remains throughout the region's parks. Volunteering at Henry Cowell helps me remain connected to my brother and allows me to enjoy his tangible legacy. Another family connection to the park is through my father, William "Bud" Osterberg, a Santa Cruz city firefighter. My father was also a wood-turner who since the 1930s made redwood novelties, which he sold to gift shops throughout California, including the park's former gift shop, known as the Burl Room.

My family helped foster within me an appreciation of the redwoods and parks. I wrote this book because I love the park and I felt compelled to share the story of this special place and to ensure that the groundbreaking role and the resort-era history of Big Trees Grove becomes more widely known and enjoyed.

ACKNOWLEDGEMENTS

Thanks to all the dedicated volunteer docents of Henry Cowell Redwoods State Park who every day share the wonders of Big Trees Grove with visitors. I'd particularly like to thank Dave Kuty and Ken Lande, from whom I first learned the grove's fascinating resort history. Thanks to Lisa Robinson, director of the San Lorenzo Valley Historical Society, for providing both images and insight on local history. The extensive knowledge of local historians Traci Bliss and Randall Brown was invaluable for better understanding the park's creation and its movie history. Jim Kliment provided stories of the Welch family and local railroad history. Sean Conly of the Genealogical Society of Santa Cruz County conducted research that put me in touch with descendants of families intimately connected to the grove's development. Though I extensively used online newspaper archives, I also located important historical information in the irreplaceable book and newspaper microfilm resources of the society's Genealogy and California History Room located in the downtown Santa Cruz Public Library.

Archival staff at institutions in the Santa Cruz area and around the country helped me obtain images, particularly Marla Novo at the Santa Cruz Museum of Art and History, Debbie Lipoma of the Santa Cruz Public Library, Pamela Nett Kruger and the Special Collections staff of California State University–Chico and Luisa Haddad and the staff of the University of California at Santa Cruz Special Collections. Many rarely seen images were obtained from private collectors. Special recognition goes to Ross Eric Gibson and Frank Perry for allowing me to explore and use some of their extensive Big Trees Grove collections. Ross was also key in helping me better understand the layout of the resort and the configuration of the long-since-gone hotel buildings. Special thanks to photographer Adria Crossen Davis for making an enhanced copy of what is believed to be the only image of Joseph Warren Welch, which was located within the Special Collections of Chico State's Meriam Library. Invaluable images were also graciously provided by Cynthia Mathews; Traci Bliss; Lynn Stewart, great-granddaughter of Milo Hopkins; and Sarah Orne Glass and the Glass family, who are descendants of Joseph Ball.

Many thanks to my former National Archives colleague Dr. Robert Glass for his historian's perspective and encouraging words. I am thankful for the sage advice from local historian and author Robert Piwarzyk. I appreciate the generosity of my former Sequoia–Kings Canyon National Parks colleague William Tweed for writing a foreword for my first book. Several friends and family, including William Greene, Lacie Gray-Lawson and Raul Yepez, also served as vital sounding boards.

Special thanks to the staff of Henry Cowell Redwoods State Park for their support and knowledgeable feedback. Steven Ellmore was key in helping update the Historic Redwood Loop Trail map. Valuable assistance with images and natural history information was also provided by Dylan McManus, Elizabeth Hammack and Jodi Apelt. The expertise of California State Park archaeologist Mark Hylkema enhanced my section related to the region's Ohlone resource management history.

I want to acknowledge Brenda Holmes, director of the Mountain Parks Foundation, and her staff for the foundation's assistance in obtaining some historic images. I began this project with the intention that it would not only fulfill a gap in the publications available about the park but also help the park in a more direct fashion. I am pleased that we were able to arrange that half the royalties from this book will be shared with Mountain Parks to help support programs at Henry Cowell Redwoods State Park.

IN THE BEGINNING

From them comes silence and awe. It's not only their unbelievable stature, nor the color which seems to shift and vary under your eyes, no, they are not like any trees we know, they are ambassadors from another time.
—*John Steinbeck,* Travels with Charley: In Search of America

The redwoods flourish along California's Coast Range from Big Sur in the south to just beyond the state's northern border. Our story takes place in the San Lorenzo Valley of the Santa Cruz Mountains, located seventy miles south of San Francisco. The granite heart of Ben Lomond Mountain forms the western edge of the valley. Overlaying the region are seismically uplifted sediments of ancient seafloors. The redwoods thrive in the valley's heavy winter rains and summer fogs. A towering grove located here at the confluence of the San Lorenzo River and Zayante Creek played a vital but little remembered role in the redwood preservation movement. These redwoods, which attained widespread fame in the late nineteenth century as Big Trees Grove, are known today as Henry Cowell Redwoods State Park.

In 1867, Joseph Warren Welch purchased about 350 acres within this grove of tall timber. Instead of logging the majestic coast redwoods, like many of his contemporaries, Welch had another plan for the Big Trees. As logging in the San Lorenzo Valley continued, Welch declared this grove of monarchs open to the public as a picnic ground, thereby making these the first coast redwoods in history to be preserved for public recreation.

The Welch family continued to manage Big Trees Grove as a resort for the next sixty years. Easily accessible by rail starting in 1875, Big Trees Grove became one of the most visited resorts in California during the late nineteenth century. The tens of thousands of tourists drawn to the grove helped spread knowledge of the redwoods and the plight they continued to face from logging. As a popular Victorian tourist destination, Big Trees Grove played a role in changing attitudes about the redwood forest. Although the trees were originally seen as either a novelty or simply a commodity due to their immense size, soon a new and growing appreciation arose for the rapidly disappearing forests and the need for their protection. An incident at Big Trees Grove around 1900 accelerated calls for preservation, later leading to the establishment of the first redwood state park, Big Basin.

> *By accident more than foresight a grove of giant red woods* [Big Trees Grove], *in the canyon of the San Lorenzo…escaped the ax. Gradually it dawned upon the people that board measure was not the only standard by which the value of trees could be computed. Thus the lines of preservation were drawn about this grove, and each year the size, beauty and majesty of these monarchs becomes more impressive, and each year they attract a large number of visitors.*
> —Arthur A. Taylor, Eastern Utah Advocate, *May 21, 1903*

Though the initial survival of this grove was more attributable to accident rather than intention, there is no doubt who should be credited for its existence today. When the Welch family decided to move on from Big Trees Grove, they followed the example of their patriarch. Just as Joseph Warren Welch first recognized the Big Trees' value to both his family and the public, his descendants eventually chose to continue his preservation legacy. In the years that followed, the selfless acts of others helped add to the grove's protection. Former Santa Cruz mayor William Jeter played an essential role in helping the grove finally attain the preservation status it deserved when it became Santa Cruz County Big Trees Park in 1930. In 1954, Samuel Cowell's generous donation of land once logged by his father was the catalyst that led to the creation of the Henry Cowell Redwoods State Park we know today. But the initial decision of Joseph Warren Welch to protect Big Trees Grove was the remarkable act that finally deserves full recognition and its proper place in the history of the preservation movement.

The First Stewards

Native people were the first stewards of this land. The Native American presence, stretching over fifteen thousand years, shaped the landscape that later European settlers would encounter. The San Lorenzo Valley was part of the homeland of the Sayant people, one of about fifty Ohlone triblelets located between the San Francisco and Monterey Bays. For the Sayant, the San Lorenzo Valley provided abundant food sources, from hazelnuts and a variety of plant bulbs and grass seeds to migrating steelhead trout, an array of fowl and herds of deer. Over the centuries, Native people used fire to expand grasslands to promote the growth of edible plants and increase forage to attract more game. The Sayant management of these resources was interrupted in 1791 with the establishment of Mission Santa Cruz.[1] The dawning of the mission era marked the removal of the first stewards from their ancestral homeland, ensuring that the lives of the Sayant people would forever change. The missionaries so depleted the Ohlone population of the Santa Cruz region that by the 1810s they began removing Yokut people from the Sierra foothills to support the Santa Cruz Mission.[2] In the 1840s, American settlers of the San Lorenzo Valley rarely encountered Native people—or so many of them thought. From the Mexican era into the American occupation, Ohlone descendants worked as farmers, ranch hands and loggers, though often concealing their true heritage to avoid the Anglo-instigated stigma about their Native roots. California's early policies formalized the enslavement of Indian children, allowed vigilante killing of Native people and prohibited the Native tradition of seasonally burning grasslands to increase foodstuffs. California's Native population was once one of the largest in North America. The huge influx of gold rush immigrants, disease and the State of California's official anti-Indian policies drastically reduced their communities. California's Native population dropped from an estimated 300,000 before European contact down to as few as 30,000 by the early twentieth century.[3]

Many descendants of the region's Native people who survived these extraordinary hardships are now represented by the Amah Mutsun tribe, the Muwekma Ohlone tribe and the Pájaro Valley Indian Council.[4] Annually since 1985, the park has hosted a September celebration of local Native culture known as Ohlone Day. In recent years, California State Park management has worked with descendants to provide new opportunities to restore some Ohlone traditional resource practices at Henry Cowell and other state parks on the Central Coast. In 2016, the Amah Mutsun tribe,

Ohlone man hunting with a bow.
Courtesy of artist Mark Hylkema, Santa Cruz District archaeologist, California State Parks.

in collaboration with archaeologists from California State Parks and the University of California, agreed to reintroduce some traditional resource management methods in the Quiroste Valley Cultural Preserve within Año Nuevo State Park.[5]

Perhaps the most visible, lasting marks of Native people's long resource stewardship history at Big Trees Grove are the broad meadow adjacent to the San Lorenzo River and the singed bark and fire-etched hollows of the redwood trunks we see today. In recent years, we have finally come to recognize the important role Native people played in creating this landscape, and it is our responsibility to join with them in the continuing stewardship of it for future generations.

RANCHOS AMONG THE REDWOODS

With the independence of Mexico in 1821, the lands of Alta California were divided and distributed as private landholdings, later known as

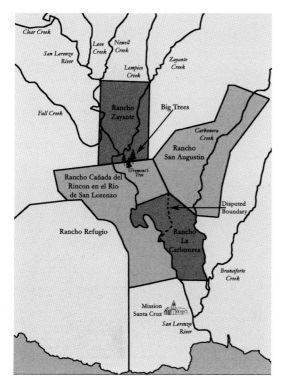

Map showing the location of Fremont's Tree in Alta California, circa 1846. *Courtesy of Lisa Robinson.*

ranchos. Henry Cowell Redwoods State Park stands at the convergence of three Mexican ranchos: Rancho Carbonera, Rancho Rincon and Rancho Zayante.[6] Perhaps the grove's location along the disputed boundaries of these ranchos contributed to its early escape from the logger's axe.

Rancho Carbonera, which bordered the San Lorenzo River north of Santa Cruz, was granted to José Guillermo Bocle in 1838.[7] Today, visitors pass along this old rancho as they drive up Highway 9 from Santa Cruz. In 1860, the lower end of Rancho Carbonera became the site of what was believed to be the first paper mill in California. Four years later, the same location became home to the California Powder Works, where high-grade, smokeless black powder was manufactured until 1916. In 1924, the site became the home of Paradise Park Masonic Club. Today, Henry Cowell Redwoods State Park stretches from that point along the lower San Lorenzo Canyon up to the town of Felton.

Rancho Rincon, which followed the western edge of the San Lorenzo Valley, was granted to French immigrant Pierre Sainsevain in 1843. The Spanish term *rincon* denotes the sharp bend that the San Lorenzo River makes, creating a steep gorge on the way up to Felton. For a short time, Sainsevain set up a sawmill on the river near what is today the park's Group Picnic Area. With the discovery of gold in 1855, the locale just upstream became known as Gold Gulch. Though the gold strike was short-lived, one story claims local settler Isaac Graham found a gold-speckled boulder that netted him approximately $30,000. Perhaps the most valuable features of Rancho Rincon were the Big Trees, which included an immense redwood that would soon attract the attention of famed explorer John Charles Frémont.

Rancho Zayante, which encompassed a portion of the northern area of the park, was granted to Joaquin Buelna in 1834. He was a former schoolteacher and served as *alcalde* (mayor) of the original Spanish pueblo of Santa Cruz, known as Villa de Branciforte. In 1835, he rented a portion of his rancho to Job Dye, who set up a gristmill and distillery. Buelna let his claim to the rancho lapse that same year, and a timber operation was begun by a couple of Americans, signaling the beginning of an expatriate American and British settlement along Zayante Creek. The presence of Dye's still may be the source of the legend that Mexican authorities dubbed the settlement "Drunkards Camp."[8] The rough company that the settlement attracted was sufficient explanation for its notoriety.

Kentucky frontiersman Isaac Graham later became one of the more well-known members of the settlement. He arrived in California in 1833 and soon earned a colorful reputation in his dealings with Mexican officials. In 1836, Graham was one of several settlers who assisted Juan Alvarado in expelling the reigning governor in what they believed was an attempt to free Alta California from Mexican authority. Later, the new governor had Graham and his associates arrested as dangerous foreign agitators. The prisoners were eventually released, with Graham receiving $36,000 as indemnity for his unjust imprisonment.

In 1842, Graham felt safe enough to return to the San Lorenzo Valley, where he met up again with Joseph Majors, who had accompanied him out to California. Majors and other settlers operated a sawmill on Zayante Creek where it enters the San Lorenzo River. Their mill was reputed to be the first power sawmill in California. Majors, who married into a Californio family, was granted Rancho Zayante.[9] Despite not being a Mexican citizen, Graham purchased rights to Rancho Zayante and the lumber mill from Majors. As the lumber business expanded, a crude road was built to transport lumber down to the ships anchored off Santa Cruz. Today, that lumber route is known as Graham Hill Road. The logging operation on Zayante Creek was just a prelude of things to come. The San Lorenzo Valley was transformed into one of the most productive lumber and lime-producing regions in what would soon become the western edge of the United States. The devastation wrought by these early resource-extracting industries transformed the landscape, focusing attention on one of the last remnants of the old-growth coast redwood forest of the San Lorenzo Valley.

An early account of an American visitor to the Big Trees of the Santa Cruz Mountains comes from a letter printed in the June 8, 1843 edition of the *Wiskonsan* (Madison) *Enquirer*. During "his exploring trip to the West," John Bartleson of the U.S. Regiment of Dragoons described the forest as containing

> *the most splendid timber I ever beheld.... The red wood has the preference for size; these trees are generally three hundred feet high. I measured one tree near Santa Cruz, about five miles from the ocean, which was fifty-nine feet in circumference, and three hundred feet without limb or knot.*[10]

The soldier's journey and astonishment at what he encountered would be repeated many times by thousands in the years to come.

Chapter 1

THE PATHFINDER AND HIS TREES

When one man, for whatever reason, has the opportunity to lead an extraordinary life, he has no right to keep it to himself.
—*Jacques Cousteau*

In May 1845, Second Lieutenant John Charles Frémont of the U.S. Army Corps of Topographical Engineers began his third scientific expedition to the West. Son-in-law of powerful U.S. senator Thomas Hart Benton, Frémont was the personification of Manifest Destiny: the belief that the expansion of the United States across North America was justified and inevitable. Frémont was one of the most celebrated explorers of nineteenth-century America. Thanks to the wilderness skills of his scout, legendary mountain man Kit Carson, and the ghostwriting and advocacy of his wife, Jessie Benton Frémont, the exciting accounts of his western mapping expeditions became bestsellers.

Frémont's destination was the continent's western coast. California, then the sparsely populated northern edge of Mexico's frontier, had a population of approximately eight thousand residents of European descent, of whom about eight hundred were expatriate Americans. The region was a long-held dream of both U.S. and British expansionists. Securing ports on the Pacific could ensure valuable trade routes to Asia. That December, U.S. president James K. Polk attempted to absolve Mexico's debts by offering to pay up to $40 million to acquire New Mexico and California. The Mexican government refused the offer about the same time Frémont arrived at Sutter's Fort in California's Sacramento Valley. Despite the fact that Frémont had initially received permission from Mexican officials to enter California, the presence of his expedition soon raised suspicions. The explorer led a sixty-man, well-armed, diverse contingent of experienced frontiersmen, scientists and soldiers, which brought into question the true character of his scientific venture.[11]

Frémont made his way down to Monterey that January to resupply and visit U.S. consul Thomas Larkin. He also assured José Castro, military commander of Alta California, that he would soon head north to complete his expedition. After a meandering trek to the Santa Clara Valley, Frémont, in violation of his promise to Castro, inexplicably turned southwest once again. Frémont's full motive for his change in plans remains a mystery. Some scholars believe he was secretly advised to discreetly obtain information about the region that could be used for possible future U.S. intervention. Ideally, the Californians could be encouraged to secede peacefully from Mexico and join the United States. Or perhaps local discontent could be fostered into revolt.

It was then February 1846, and once again in pursuit of their scientific duties, Frémont's expedition, guided by Kit Carson, traveled to the Santa Cruz Mountains. In his memoirs, Frémont explained:

> *The accounts of the great trees in the forest on the west slope of the mountain had roused my curiosity....Among many we measured in this part of the mountain a diameter of nine or ten feet was frequent, sometimes eleven…*[including] *a single tree, which reached fourteen feet in diameter. Above two hundred feet was a frequent height. In this locality the bark was very deeply furrowed and unusually thick, being fully sixteen inches on some of the trees....Posts which had been exposed to the weather three-quarters of a century, since the foundation of the Missions, showed no marks of decay in the wood and are now converted into beams and posts for private dwellings.*[12]

The expedition spent a portion of its time in the San Lorenzo Valley at Rancho Zayante, home of frontiersman Isaac Graham. A confederate from Carson's fur trapping days, Graham was a member of the small logging settlement along Zayante Creek and served as Frémont's host. In addition to taking a closer look at the redwoods, this was also a good opportunity to collect plan specimens for Frémont's friend John Torrey, a prominent Princeton botanist.[13] This stop would also allow Frémont's men to replenish

Left: John Charles Frémont, taken by Samuel Root. Salted paper print, circa 1856. *Courtesy of the National Portrait Gallery, Smithsonian Institution.*

Below: The last Rancho Zayante tanning vat washed away in the 1955 flood of the San Lorenzo River. *Courtesy of the Santa Cruz Museum of Art and History.*

their leather goods after the long trek. A primitive tannery operated on Graham's rancho. Using four large troughs, about three feet across and twelve feet long, cut from a single giant redwood, settlers tanned bear skins and deer hides.[14]

Graham took the explorer on a tour of his rancho. Frémont was immediately impressed and declared that the redwoods' "colossal height and massive bulk give an air of grandeur to the forest." Since Frémont was captivated by the enormous stature of the redwoods, Graham asked him to measure the largest. Frémont took several days to complete his work, stating later that "I measured one which was two hundred and seventy-five feet in height and fifteen feet in diameter, three feet above the base." In thanks for the statistics Frémont provided, Graham is said to have honored the explorer by carving a letter *F* into the tree's bark, thereby christening it Frémont's Tree.[15] Since then, growth of bark and some later episodes of vandalism have obscured the marking, making it indistinguishable today.

After several weeks' stay, Frémont's expedition resumed its progress, but instead of heading out of California, they once again traveled toward Monterey. Frémont received a message from Castro ordering him to leave the region immediately. Frémont responded by setting up hasty fortifications on the side of Gavilán Peak (now known as Fremont Peak), where he raised an American flag. Soon, Castro had assembled three hundred volunteers below the American defenses. With tensions growing, a fortuitous event occurred. On March 9, Frémont's makeshift flagpole fell over, which he took as an omen that he should make a strategic withdrawal. He later said that he kept "always in mind the object of the Government to obtain possession of California and would not let a proceeding which was mostly personal put obstacles in the way."[16] Feeling vindicated and secure in his dignity, he easily withdrew.

The expedition finally headed northward. On April 5, 1846, about half the members of Frémont's expedition joined local settlers in a raid on an Indian village located near present-day Redding. The motive of the attack, known as the Sacramento River Massacre, remains in dispute. Locals said the raid was launched to prevent a believed impending Indian attack on settlers. Expedition member Thomas E. Breckenridge of the Topographical Engineers, who claimed not to have participated in the attack, described how his colleagues and local settlers charged into the village, "taking the warriors by surprise and then commenced a scene of slaughter which is unequalled in the West. The bucks, squaws and paposes were shot down like sheep and those men never stopped as long as they could find one alive."[17] Though

Frémont claimed only 14 Indians were killed, other accounts estimated that the merciless attack killed from 175 to as many as 700 Wintu and Yana people, mostly women and children, and set an ominous tone for the coming American settlement of California.[18]

Soon after the massacre, Frémont was reached by a courier, U.S. Marine Corps lieutenant Archibald H. Gillespie. Disguised as an ailing merchant, Gillespie carried confidential messages informing the explorer of the current political situation. A surviving letter from Secretary of State James Buchanan stated, "In the contest between Mexico and California…we can take no part…but should California assert and maintain her independence, we shall render her all kind of offices in our power, as a sister republic."[19] That hope soon became reality. Encouraged by Frémont's presence in the region, a few dozen American settlers from the pueblo of Sonoma started a revolt against Mexican authority on their own on June 10, 1846. Their ire was sparked by a recent proclamation from José Castro declaring that those settlers who did not become citizens of Mexico, as prescribed by law, would have their land purchases revoked. The rebels quickly raised their flag of independence: one adorned with a rather awkward-looking grizzly bear. The flag also bore a red star apparently as a tribute to Texas, which had won its independence from Mexico a decade earlier. When word of the Bear Flag Revolt reached Frémont, he hurried to the site and quickly became the Bear Flaggers' unofficial advisor. Unbeknownst to the rebels, the United States had declared war on Mexico over a month earlier.[20] Once word of the war arrived, Frémont continued to lead many of the same rebels in battle for the United States. Commodore Robert Stockton, in charge of U.S. forces in California at the advent of the Mexican War, appointed Frémont military governor. Upon his arrival in California, General Stephen W. Kearny took command and quickly came into conflict with Frémont, whom he soon had court-martialed for mutiny. Though he was convicted, the sentence was set aside by President Polk. Disheartened by the episode, Frémont resigned from the army. But in the minds of the American people, he was the Conqueror of California.[21]

After the war, Frémont hoped to purchase a ranch near the beautiful Santa Cruz Mountains he first traversed as an explorer. When called out of state, he gave $3,280 to his friend Thomas Larkin to make a purchase. Instead of obtaining land in the Santa Cruz area, Larkin bought Las Mariposas Grant in the dry Sierra foothills. Frémont was initially upset with Larkin's choice. But with the discovery of gold on the rancho in 1848, Frémont soon learned he owned one of the richest properties in California.[22]

When California gained statehood in 1850, Frémont's fame continued to grow as he became one of the new state's first U.S. senators. Frémont was the first Republican nominee for president in 1856 and later served as a general during the Civil War. As the first Republican presidential candidate, Frémont opposed both the western expansion of slavery and the existence of polygamy. During the Civil War, he served in Missouri as major general in charge of the Department of the West. In August 1861, without notifying President Lincoln, Frémont issued a proclamation freeing the slaves in the region. President Lincoln quickly overruled Frémont's premature effort at emancipation.

One of Frémont's most enduring contributions to California took place on July 1, 1846, when he described the entrance to San Francisco Bay as "a golden gate to trade with the Orient."[23] Though throughout his life Frémont's fortunes and fame would fluctuate, the nation's fascination with the man and his exploits endured. The association of the Frémont name with a mammoth redwood in the San Lorenzo Valley bolstered the fortunes of the later Big Trees Grove resort and appears to be the initial reason the grove survived to become the park we enjoy today.

A TALE OF TWO BIG TREES

The Big Trees of the San Lorenzo Valley entered the nation's consciousness through the expedition narrative of famed explorer John Charles Frémont. Though the *ho-o-pe* were known to the Sayant people for thousands of years and described by the Spanish as *palo colorado* since the 1769 Portolá expedition,[24] Frémont's descriptions of the Big Trees were initially met with disbelief by his fellow Americans. Soon skepticism was replaced with fascination. In 1851, a Vermont newspaper told readers that in "Frémont's Memoirs of Upper California, we find some accounts of the forest trees of that country, which, if the statements were not vouched for by good authority, we should class them with the stories of Baron Munchausen."[25] Multiplying tales of Frémont's adventures in California would eventually lead thousands of tourists to "Frémont's Grove" to follow in the footsteps of the famed explorer and hero of the Bear Flag Revolt and Mexican War. Soon after Frémont's sojourn, small parties of tourists began making their way to see "Fremont's saplings" for themselves.[26]

We found it [Fremont's Tree]…*surrounded by a forest of the same kind of trees, of less yet of gigantic growth. We immediately commenced measuring with a tapeline, carried with us for that purpose, and found the tree to measure, two feet from the ground, fifty-two feet in circumference; its average diameter is seventeen feet.…We estimated the hight to be three hundred feet.…It is surrounded by many other trees of great hight and from eight to twelve feet in diameter; this place forms the resort of frequent pic-nic parties. We are informed by Capt. Graham that on his farm existed trees of still larger dimensions.*[27]

Such excursions, as this one in 1856, set the pattern of all those that would follow: tourists coming to picnic under the shade of the towering redwoods and to marvel at the gigantic dimensions of its most noble residents.

The earliest known artist's rendition of Fremont's Tree was by Edward Vischer and published in his 1870 *Vischer's Pictorial of California Landscape, Trees, and Forest Scenes: Grand Features of California Scenery, Life, Traffic, and Customs.*[28] By 1852, the Bavarian-born Vischer had established an import business in San Francisco, where he began sketching California's magnificent landscapes as a hobby. Most noted for his lithographs of the giant sequoias of the Sierra Nevada, Vischer also made his way down to the Santa Cruz Mountains.[29] In November 1862, the *Santa Cruz Weekly Sentinel* wrote, "The gentleman who sketched the Big Trees of Calaveras, and of Washoe, paid the Santa Cruz trees a visit this week for that purpose."[30] In his pictorial, the artist described Fremont's Tree as "the noblest scion" of the giant grove.[31] Vischer also noted a nearby redwood with a fire-hollowed base and recounted the local lore that

a family was housed for a winter, and evidences of that fact are still visible. There was no lack of room for such an occupation of it. Thirty men might stand up in it at once, and many more be stowed away about near the ground. It must have been rather a gloomy home, for the only chance for light and air is at the entrance, which is barely large enough for a person to walk through.[32]

The earliest known newspaper account of the hollow tree in the grove appeared in an August 27, 1860 article in the *Daily Alta California*. The correspondent also referred to local lore, stating that adjacent to Fremont's Tree stood "another large tree of the same kind, but hollow. In this hollow tree a family dwelt all winter and kept two borders [*sic*]."[33]

Fremont's Tree (now known as the Giant), by Edward Vischer, 1862. *Edward Vischer Papers, Special Collections, Honnold/Mudd Library of Claremont Colleges.*

Soon another story began to circulate. The new story claimed that during his 1846 expedition, Frémont slept within the fire-scarred hollow of a giant redwood. The origin of the account is uncertain. Some attribute it to Frémont's wife, Jessie Benton Frémont, who assisted her husband in preparing his expedition journals for publication. Fremont's Tree, which its namesake measured, did not fit the new narrative. The tallest Big Tree in the grove was not hollow. Standing within a stone's throw of Fremont's Tree, however, was the redwood with the immense, fire-carved hollow at its base, which began to draw more visitor attention. At some point, the two stories merged. The earliest known printed association of Frémont's story and this hollow redwood was made in the August 1, 1868 edition of the *Santa Cruz Times*, which described the hollow tree as "the camping place of the great pathfinder of the American continent, John C. Frémont, in the Bear Flag times."[34] As time passed, the tree originally measured by Frémont would become known simply as the Giant, and the nearby hollow tree became the Fremont Tree we know today. The question of whether John Charles Frémont ever slept within the hollow of this tree would be saved for another day.

AXES AND LIMEKILNS

The first primitive logging operations in the San Lorenzo Valley up through the 1830s used whipsawing pits, which took two men an entire day to cut about one hundred feet of lumber.[35] In the years following Frémont's sojourn through the coast redwoods, the San Lorenzo Valley became an epicenter of California's early lumber industry. Soon the pace of logging accelerated with the advent of mechanical, water-powered sawmills. The lumber need generated by the gold rush and the growth of San Francisco made redwood a highly valuable commodity. This intense demand was anxiously fulfilled by the lumbermen of the Santa Cruz Mountains. By the late 1860s, the San Lorenzo Valley supported twenty-two lumber mills with an annual capacity of eleven million board feet of lumber.[36] The town of Felton, founded in 1868, was the scene of teams "constantly arriving, loaded with tan-bark, lumber, lime, cord wood, powder wood, pickets, posts, shingle belts, and stave bolts."[37] In 1874 alone, San Francisco used eighty-seven million board feet of redwood lumber for construction.[38] By the early twentieth century, the clear-cutting of redwood had one visitor describe the stump-filled San Lorenzo

Valley as a "Black Tombstone Cemetery."[39] Today, less than 5 percent of all the old-growth redwoods that stood before 1849 are still living.[40]

An even more valuable resource extracted from the valley was limestone. Lime was an essential ingredient in the making of mortar and plaster. Limestone found in the Santa Cruz Mountains was considered some of the purest in the nation, and the mortar made with it helped build and rebuild San Francisco. Limestone was reduced by heating it in stone kilns that were kept at temperatures up to two thousand degrees Fahrenheit.[41] As early as the mid-1870s, the lime industry near Felton employed about one hundred men. Redwood served as the primary source of kiln fuel, with a single Big Tree able to provide over one hundred cords. From six to thirteen cords of wood were needed to produce one hundred barrels of lime. Throughout the 1890s, the combined limekilns of the Santa Cruz Mountains annually produced approximately 150,000 barrels of lime using as much as twenty thousand cords of wood, further decimating the old-growth forests.[42]

THE LIME BARON

The most successful lime entrepreneur and a man who left a lasting imprint on the San Lorenzo Valley was Henry Cowell. Born in 1819 on a Massachusetts farm, Cowell came to California during the gold rush. He and his brother John quickly found success by opening a hauling business. In 1865, Henry spent $100,000 to purchase part of the Jordan and Davis lime works in the Santa Cruz Mountains. By 1888, he had taken control, and he eventually named it the Henry Cowell Lime and Cement Company. His businesses were far-ranging and very profitable and soon made him one of the richest men in Santa Cruz.[43] Cowell was a very private man and did not care for members of the media, whom he called the "irresponsible, rotten, mercenary press." Many of his self-serving business practices caused a rift between him and his neighbors, and he often became involved in legal disputes.[44] The general opinion of Cowell was not kind:

No man can accumulate wealth as Cowell has accumulated it without giving many people the impression that he has wronged them. Henry Cowell is one of the strictly unsentimental class of millionaires. He conceives the joy of living to be the accumulation and hoarding of money....[He] is never guilty of ostentatious display and wears clothes that are spotted...but

Henry Cowell made a fortune through lumber and lime operations in the San Lorenzo Valley. *Courtesy of the Santa Cruz Museum of Art and History.*

Felton, circa 1910. Barren hillsides attest to the intensive redwood logging throughout the nineteenth century. *Courtesy of the Santa Cruz Museum of Art and History.*

he is tight-fisted and drives a hard bargain. And they say that although he owned half the timber land in the county, if one of his employees took home a stick of wood, and Cowell found it out, he would deduct the price from the man's wages. No doubt many stories of Cowell's charity could be told, but unfortunately, they have never been recorded.[45]

In the 1870s, Cowell bought into the IXL Lime Company located along Fall Creek, just west of Felton. In 1900, he became sole owner of the kilns, which continued to operate until 1919. During their peak in the 1890s, these kilns produced fifty thousand barrels of lime per year.[46] Thanks to the S.H. Cowell Foundation, remnants of the kilns became part of Henry Cowell Redwoods State Park in 1972.[47]

Cowell eventually acquired about ten thousand acres in and around Santa Cruz County, including land within a few hundred feet of the campsite of Frémont's famed 1846 expedition. By 1900, Cowell began logging his side of the San Lorenzo River, cutting his gigantic redwoods into kiln fuel. Seeing the destruction of the forest monarchs, one observer lamented, "There is no poetry in some men's composition."[48] But changes were coming. Transportation routes built to extract the region's resource wealth would soon become the conduits for a burgeoning tourism industry stretching from Santa Cruz's last remaining old-growth redwood groves to its scenic coastline.

Chapter 2

PRESERVATION BEGINS

JOSEPH WARREN WELCH AND HIS PICNIC GROUND

It's not what you look at that matters, it's what you see.
—Henry David Thoreau

In the summer of 1867, a fire, attributed to a careless fishing party, raged through the Santa Cruz Mountains.

> *The dark and heavy cloud of smoke, which obscures the horizon in the direction of the Sayante is truly an ominous sight....At the Powder works, one of the employees informs us, flakes of fire, as large as a man's hand were flying through the air and dropping in close proximity to the works.*[49]

At this time, the remains of Isaac Graham's old rancho were up for sale. At Graham's death in 1863, the grove came into the possession of attorney Edward Stanly in compensation for legal services he rendered the old pioneer. Stanly probably intended to sell off the property for a good profit to local logging interests, but recent fire damage may have deterred some prospective buyers. A San Francisco acquaintance of Stanly's, Joseph Warren Welch, showed interest in the grove, even bringing his family down for a campout under the trees.[50] In December 1867, Welch purchased about 350 acres of this timber land located at the confluence of the San Lorenzo River and Zayante Creek for $8,750.[51] One story claims that he surprised his family with the news on Christmas Day.[52] Under Welch's ownership, about 40 acres of this parcel, containing dozens of mammoth coast redwoods, was soon to be known worldwide as Big Trees Grove.

Despite his importance to the grove's story, precious little is known about Joseph Warren Welch or his motives. He was a native of Massachusetts, coming to California during the gold rush in 1849. He tried his hand at mining for a few months but, like many contemporaries, quickly learned that success in California meant getting out of the mines and into a business providing services to others. Welch moved to San Francisco and became a carrier of one of California's first newspapers, the *Daily Alta California*. In 1852, he married Anna Learned, and they soon began a family.[53] He worked for the newspaper for twenty-five years, earning a comfortable livelihood.[54] According to the 1870 federal census, Welch's real estate was valued at $47,500. Today, that would amount to approximately $900,000.

As a newspaper carrier, the fifty-one-year-old Welch was likely well acquainted with the stories of John Charles Frémont's travels and military exploits, including his brief sojourn among the redwoods of the Santa Cruz Mountains. Perhaps those stories influenced his decision to buy the grove. Coincidentally, for many years, the Welch family resided on Rincon Hill at 434 Fremont Street in San Francisco.[55] Though both Welch and Frémont resided in the city during a portion of the 1860s, there is no proof they ever met. One story claimed that Anna's love of the trees persuaded her husband to purchase the grove.[56] We may never know all the reasons why Welch chose to buy the grove of monumental trees, but the importance

This 1875 photograph by Romanzo E. Wood is believed to be of (*right to left*) Joseph Warren Welch Sr., Joseph Welch Jr., Stanly Welch and Herman Welch. *Courtesy of the R.E. Wood Collection, Meriam Library Special Collections, California State University, Chico. Image photographed and enhanced by Adria Crossen Davis.*

of his decision is undisputed. The grove was already known as a "picnic ground romantic and charming, the Summer resort of pleasure-seekers visiting Santa Cruz."[57] Welch realized the tourist potential engendered by one of the last stands of old-growth redwoods in the Santa Cruz Mountains, and his purchase of the grove ensured it would be preserved and remain open to the public.

It is unclear whether Welch realized that he was making history when he chose to protect Big Trees Grove. By keeping the grove open to visitors, Welch was the first to save a coast redwood forest from the logger's axe purely for public enjoyment. Welch was part of a larger change in American society taking place in the nineteenth century. Gradually, people began to enjoy more leisure time and disposable income. Spending time amid spectacular natural scenery furnished an opportunity for sorely needed relaxation. The new nature tourism provided both wealthy and middle-class Americans with an outlet from stressful changes brought on by increasing urbanization and industrialization. The setting aside of Big Trees Grove in 1867 came very early in our nation's nascent efforts in nature preservation, only a few years after the reserving of Yosemite Valley and the Mariposa Grove of Big Trees (1864); before the establishment of our nation's first national park, Yellowstone (1872); and thirty-five years before the establishment of the first redwood state park, Big Basin (1902).

A picnic party poses in front of the Three Sisters. Note the American flags draped above the entrance to the Fremont Tree. *Courtesy of Ross Eric Gibson.*

The Big Trees Grove story also fits within the American tradition of boosterism about our natural wonders. Early promoters boasted of our young nation's unique landscapes as a counterpoint to the much older and revered natural and cultural landmarks of Europe and the Middle East. Throughout the nineteenth century, traveling to see America's wonders was advocated by many over traveling across the ocean to see the Old World. This new nature tourism industry, steeped in a sense of patriotism, contributed to our evolving attitudes toward the natural world. Visiting landscapes made famous by a frontier and military hero like John Charles Frémont was in line with the national desire for pride in our young nation's accomplishments.[58]

> *The excursion to the big trees, in the grove near Felton, where Gen. Fremont once camped, is one of the most attractive trips for summer sojourners in Santa Cruz. Nearly everyday visitors make up picnic parties to enjoy the ride through one of the most picturesque portions of this region.*[59]

Though the grove attracted many wealthy and upper-middle-class residents from the San Francisco Bay Area and beyond, it was also a top recreational draw for locals, particularly as a site for convention and group picnics, special events and dances.

Ho! For the Big Trees!

For many years, the road from Santa Cruz to Felton was the steep-graded, dangerous logging road originally built by Isaac Graham. Starting around 1866, locals sought a better route for hauling freight between the mills of the San Lorenzo Valley and the shipping wharf in Santa Cruz. Cut along the west bank of the San Lorenzo River Canyon, the new road was an engineering marvel. It wound "around precipices which fall sheer three or four hundred feet to the bed of the creek below. Expert driving is required to get in safety around the frequent and sharp turns."[60] Funds to build the six-mile road were raised by subscription, and tolls were raised for maintenance.[61] Soon the new route became known as Big Trees Road. The road allowed easier access to Big Trees Grove for tourists, with only an hour's carriage drive from Santa Cruz.[62] It still took many hours for stagecoach operators to bring visitors from San Jose over any of the several difficult, winding routes over the Santa Cruz Mountains. One of the prominent stagecoach operators during

View of the swinging bridge over the San Lorenzo River at the original entrance to Big Trees Grove, circa 1880s. *Courtesy of Ross Eric Gibson.*

the 1870s was George L. Colegrove. For the tourist trade, he operated what was known as a "Yosemite wagon," which afforded well-padded seats for the wealthy San Franciscans who came on chartered sightseeing trips. Realizing his stage business would decline with the advent of rail service over the hill in 1880, Colegrove eventually began working for the railroad.[63]

During these early years, carriages from Santa Cruz turned off the main road at the Toll House to reach the San Lorenzo River. Stages then forded the shallow, gravelly riverbed, while their passengers disembarked to traverse a natural bridge formed by a fallen redwood tree.[64] Railings were added and the curved top leveled for easier access. Over the years, this primitive bridge was followed by a succession of suspension bridges.[65] One party's crossing of a later suspension bridge was described by a British tourist:

> *The river was wide, and there we saw, slung across at a height of about fifteen feet, fixed from high bank to bank, a narrow footway consisting of long, thin, single, narrow planks, attached to each other end by end, with a single rope, of tolerable thickness, stretched as a kind of banister, at a height of about five feet above the plank bridge, but unconnected with it, attached to two "big trees," opposite each other, on each bank of the river!... The frail single planking began to bounce violently up and down, although we crept along as slowly and carefully as possible!...Joy! joy! that fearful obstacle passed!....Now nothing to do but to delight and revel in the marvel, the wonder, of these most extraordinary trees!*[66]

Replacement of the suspension bridge became a recurring expense due to frequent flooding. The mild summer personality of the San Lorenzo River is deceiving. In 1878, an early pedestrian bridge was washed out when spring floodwaters reached twenty-seven feet deep.[67]

Once on the other side of the river, visitors passed through a log cabin, the interior of which was plastered with visitors' business and personal calling cards.[68] Visitors originally entered the grove near the Giant, which is the approximate midpoint of today's Redwood Loop Trail. Young ladies would often stop at the river, removing their shoes and stockings to bathe their ankles in the cool water. One such scene at the riverside was amusingly described in an account of tourists visiting Big Trees Grove in a June 13, 1874 *Santa Cruz Weekly Sentinel* article titled "Fremont's Saplings":

> *The Naiads who sport in the waters of the San Lorenzo never get mad unless some senseless wandering brute of An Awful Man comes blindly*

perambulating into sight and then they scream…and scramble frantically for the dry land.

Gentlemen who go on picnic excursions to the big trees are admonished of the consequences of going near the banks of the stream while the waters are being agitated by feminine ankles. They will find themselves on forbidden ground, and what is more they will have a hard afternoon's work to affect a reconciliation with the Offended Beauties.

Sacramento, Stockton, and Marysville girls don't mind it a bit. San Francisco and Auburn maids will work themselves into a gentle fury from which they soon recover; but a Truckee girl will neither forgive nor forget the atrocity of a man contemplating the philosophy of a well-turned ankle.[69]

Along the edge of the San Lorenzo River, the area shaded by laurels, white alders and towering sycamores was once known as Idlewild Glade.[70] Visitors pass through this historic glade when walking today's River Trail from the Group Picnic Area.

Visitors refresh themselves in the shallow water of the San Lorenzo River at the entrance to Big Trees Grove, circa 1900. *Courtesy of Ross Eric Gibson.*

64 ft. in Circumference, 307 ft. in Height.   [OVER]

A circa 1880s Pacific Ocean House advertisement featured Santa Cruz's most important tourist destinations, its ocean cliffs and the famous Big Trees Grove. *Author's personal collection.*

The development of Big Trees Grove was concurrent with tourist attractions and accommodations springing up along the Santa Cruz coastline. Many early tourist guides recommended visitors combine a trip to Big Trees Grove with a leisurely carriage ride along Cliff Road to view wave-sculpted sandstone cliffs and mudstone arches. Soon, locals were boasting of the medicinal benefits of saltwater bathing. By 1868, the Leibrandt family had opened the first hot saltwater plunge on the West Coast.[71] Starting in 1900, Santa Cruz began to attract nearly 100,000 visitors annually. Entrepreneur Fred Swanton, determined to make Santa Cruz the "Coney Island of the West," was the most prolific and successful at building accommodations and amusement facilities along the beachfront. His construction of Neptune's Casino in 1904 was the genesis of the Boardwalk we enjoy today.[72]

Word of Big Trees Grove continued to spread. Despite its growing popularity, little is known about the early day-to-day management of the picnic ground. Welch seems to have spent little time at the grove, preferring instead to live in San Francisco. An 1873 Vermont newspaper article titled "A House in California One Thousand Years Old" described a visitor's encounter with a grove resident. It is uncertain whether the unnamed man

Girls pose beneath the Three Sisters. Note the steps to the bandstand situated among the Nine Muses in the background. *Courtesy of Frank Perry*.

was an interloper or serving as a caretaker, but the identity of his dwelling was undoubtably the Fremont Tree.

Fire had eaten away the trunk at the base, until a circular room had been formed sixteen feet in diameter. At twenty feet or more from the ground was a knothole, which afforded egress for the smoke. With hammocks hung from pegs, and a few cooking utensils hung upon other pegs, that house lacked no essential thing. This woodman was in possession of a house which had been a thousand years in process of building.[73]

At the conclusion of the visit, the unnamed occupant of the Fremont Tree made a specific request of the curious visitor: "I reckon if you are going back to town, you might tell Jim to send me up a gallon of whisky, and some plug tobacco."[74] Identity of the man remains a mystery. An early account claimed Moses Meder lived for a time within the Fremont Tree while building a sawmill for Isaac Graham.[75] By 1854, Meder had established a ranch along the Santa Cruz coast that today is the site of Wilder Ranch State Park. An account in October 1875 stated that the hollow tree was once the home of an old hunter named Jacob R. Snyder of Sonoma. While in the Santa Cruz Mountains, Snyder reported an interesting encounter with a different kind of forest dweller:

One day so runs the tale, Jacob, while meandering through the sylvan groves, felt a heavy hand laid on his shoulder, and looking around saw a gigantic grizzly grinning in his face. Jacob's blood, all ran down into his toes. He muttered a reverent prayer to that Divine Being, who can only grant assistance in cases of this kind, and then stealthily raised his gun. But the grizzly said, as plainly as grizzlies can and do say, sometimes, "Old fellow, it won't do, I've got the bulge on you, and the best thing you can do is to be not quite so reckless and careless. I've got you, Jacob." But Jacob didn't know about that. He was well aware that he was in a desperate situation, which was growing more and more desperate every moment. At this juncture, however, a happy idea struck him. Jacob chewed tobacco, and at that moment had a large quid of that necessary weed in his mouth and a mouthful of red-hot saliva. As the grizzly was on the point of converting Jacob into mincemeat, the old hunter, taking deliberate aim, spirted a jet of the fiery fluid into each of his ursine majesty's eyes. The bear roared and bellowed in pain and, blinded by the juice, floundered about aimlessly, in which helpless state he was soon dispatched.[76]

Grizzly bears were once the dominant predator in the Santa Cruz Mountains. The California grizzly could exceed two thousand pounds, making it more than twice the size of the Yellowstone grizzly. Because the bounty of California allowed the bears to feed all year long, they had no need to hibernate. They once ranged between the redwoods and the coastline feeding on acorns, berries, roots, deer, fish and even whales. The last grizzlies were seen in the Santa Cruz Mountains in the 1890s, though some may have survived near Big Basin after 1900. As a consequence of hunting, the California grizzly bear was officially declared extinct by the early 1920s. Today, the largest predator that traverses the park is the mountain lion.[77] Now the most well-known and frequently seen denizen of the grove is the Pacific banana slug. Despite its popularity with today's visitors, no known historical visitor accounts took notice of this colorful creature.

Chapter 3

JOURNEY TO THE BIG TREES

For since the world began,
And San Lorenzo ran,
Was never scene so lovely
Displayed to mortal man.
—Daily Alta California, *July 5, 1880*

Though the toll road to Felton was well traveled, its 10 percent grade was still a problem for hauling freight. The first effort to build a railroad through San Lorenzo Canyon in the 1860s failed due to lingering legal questions related to the old Mexican ranchos and the uncertainty of the ongoing Civil War. Success finally came with the completion of the narrow-gauge Santa Cruz & Felton Railroad in 1875.[78] A visitor to Big Trees Grove described the rail journey in 1877:

The cars start from the depot, near the wharves, and run along the outskirts of town to a point directly opposite and below the Court house, when they enter a tunnel of 1,000 feet, through Mission hill, upon which the county buildings are situated, the cars passing directly under the county jail. Emerging from the opposite side of the hill, which shuts out most of Santa Cruz from view, we see below us the pretty gardens and dwellings which border San Lorenzo river, and we rapidly glide along into the wildest glens and rugged mountain scenery imaginable....Running as it does along the side of a steep mountain, its course is tortuous, and the outlook suggestive

Entrance of the Santa Cruz & Felton Railroad tunnel under Mission Hill, circa 1880s.
Courtesy of the Santa Cruz Museum of Art and History.

of danger to the nervously inclined. We pass over trestle work in several places, and one is 95 feet above the canyon, which it spans, and is 500 feet long....Gigantic trees, shrubs with dense foliage, deep water-worn gorges, bold mountain projections, the river-washed ravine far below, altogether form a sublime picture of nature in her wildest and most fantastic moods.[79]

Due to the difficult mountainous terrain, the route cost $15,000 per mile. Along its eight-and-a-half-mile length were twenty-three bridges. Several of the trestles were erected on mountainsides, and the supporting uprights were imbedded into solid rock.[80]

One of the views most commented on by visitors on the way to the grove was the California Powder Works, two miles outside Santa Cruz. Most admired was the stately home of Powder Works superintendent B. Payton, which was situated on a bluff overlooking the San Lorenzo River. Originally, passengers arrived at the Felton Depot, from which they either walked or took a carriage to Big Trees Grove. Along the tracks between the grove and the depot was the rail yard and the San Lorenzo flume. Built by the railroad company, the flume was a marvel of engineering. Sawn logs and shingles were floated down from Boulder Creek–area lumber mills, thirteen miles distant. The flume carried "250 square inches of water [with]...a capacity of floating 100,000 feet of lumber per day" and operated until 1885.[81]

Early on, the railroad erected a fence at the toll road entrance to the grove, claiming the move was to prevent wandering cattle from delaying

The Santa Cruz & Felton Railroad crosses a trestle on the way to Big Trees Grove. *Courtesy of the Santa Cruz Museum of Art & History.*

the trains. Cattle on the tracks brought traffic to a halt several times a month. Some locals felt that the fence was put up primarily to make access to Big Trees Grove more difficult by wagon, thereby forcing more people to patronize the railroad.[82]

In 1959, railroad enthusiast F. Norman Clark leased 180 acres of land in Felton from Welch family descendants. By 1963, Clark had transformed the property, adjacent to Henry Cowell Redwoods State Park, into the western theme park now known as Roaring Camp Narrow Gauge Railroad. In an effort to preserve part of the region's rail history, Clark also acquired portions of the historic Southern Pacific rail line. In 1986, Clark's widow, Georgianna, obtained the rights to operate on this line, which is part of the original route of the Santa Cruz & Felton and the South Pacific Coast Railroads.[83] Today, tourists who travel from Felton to the Santa Cruz Boardwalk aboard Roaring Camp's Big Trees & Pacific Railroad are riding the historic route that brought tens of thousands of visitors to Big Trees Grove.

Chapter 4

A RESORT SPROUTS IN THE FOREST

The identity of this beautiful and historical spot is lost in some instances in published articles by its early visitors…because of not having been given a singular title.…Anyone or any group going to the Big Trees by foot, horse or train—this was the place, no further explanation was necessary.
—*Phyllis Patten, Santa Cruz historian and author,* Santa Cruz Sentinel, *January 11, 1959*

Joseph Warren Welch passed away in November 1875 at the age of fifty-nine.[84] He spent only eight years as proprietor of his picnic ground among the redwoods. But in that short time, the name "Big Trees Grove" became famous, and that fame would only continue to grow in the years to follow. Welch left his property to his wife, Anna, for the support of their five children: Joseph Jr., Herman, Isabella, I. Douglas[85] and Stanly. Welch's estate was valued at about $100,000, which today would be just over $2 million.[86] Welch's most important legacy for his family and, as it turned out also for future generations, was the grove itself.

The Welch family retained ownership of the Big Trees but entrusted development and day-to-day operation of the grove to lessees. On May 12, 1876, John Mackintire Hooper, also known as Major Hooper, was the first to have a tenancy at Big Trees Grove.[87] According to the 1880 U.S. federal census, Hooper was born in Massachusetts in 1826. Unfortunately, little else is known about his life before Big Trees Grove.

View of the Giant taken by Carleton Watkins, circa 1880s. *Digital image courtesy of the Getty's Open Content Program, J. Paul Getty Museum, Los Angeles.*

Since most visitors still arrived in carriages, Hooper's first order of business was to improve the road crossing of the San Lorenzo River, making the crossing less steep.[88] He boasted that the road was sprinkled daily and entirely free from dust.[89] Visitors came in carriages of four to ten passengers each, whose drivers provided picnic lunches of coffee and beefsteak.[90] A railroad contractor described the grove as the most beautiful picnic ground he'd ever seen:

> *Surrounded by mountains, wooded to the extreme tops, it appears as though nature had originally intended it as a harbor of peace and refuge for care-laden men desirous of retiring from the busy world for a season, and whilst resting the troubled mind to be drawn to a consideration of the wonders of nature's handiwork and to the omnipotence of nature's God.*[91]

The coming of the railroad probably helped Hooper make his decision to manage Big Trees Grove. The inaugural trip of the Santa Cruz & Felton Railroad in October 1875 was celebrated at the grove with roasted mussels for over 2,500 passengers.[92]

Under Hooper's management, Big Trees Grove evolved from a simple picnic ground to a true resort. He cleared underbrush, created the first winding walkways and built rustic seats, arbors, tables and benches. Carriage drives and bridle paths were laid out, some of which led to large trees never before seen by visitors until their discovery by Hooper.[93] He also built a rustic bower known as the Arcade or Parlor, a redwood stump covered with an octagon-shaped gazebo with seating for fourteen.[94] Most significantly,

The Big Trees Grove hotel built by John Hooper, circa 1876. *Courtesy of the R.E. Wood Collection, Meriam Library Special Collections, California State University–Chico.*

For many years, the Giant wore "a great corset of cards" tacked there by tourists. *Santa Cruz Public Libraries*.

Hooper constructed the first hotel building at Big Trees Grove. The simple wooden structure near the Fremont Tree appeared to contain up to six rooms and a kitchen. Mary Hooper, "a large, fleshy woman,"[95] began to offer visitors breakfasts, dinners and hot and cold lunches. You could also "purchase great bumbers of ice-cream at ten cents a dish."[96] The *Santa Cruz Weekly Sentinel* proclaimed the "present lessee of the grove is obliging and does all in his power to make visitors comfortable, and is always prepared to cook such meals as may be required, from the regular beef steak and chop to the expensive chicken dinner."[97]

The most popular innovations made by Hooper were construction of a dance floor and bandstand near the Giant. The dance floor measured approximately forty by fifty feet[98] and could accommodate sixteen sets of dancers.[99] Hooper's intention was to give three moonlight parties per month during the summer. The new Santa Cruz & Felton Railroad consented to run excursion trains for the dances, and Hooper promised that "ice cream, strawberries, in fact, refreshments of all kinds, will be kept constantly on hand."[100] The first grand moonlight ball at Big Trees Grove was given on

A couple near the dance floor by Carleton Watkins, circa 1880s. *Digital image courtesy of Getty's Open Content Program, J. Paul Getty Museum, Los Angeles.*

May 24, 1877. A charge of two dollars covered both the round-trip fare and supper. Music for the inaugural dance was provided by Littlefield's Quadrille Band,[101] with sixty couples in attendance dancing under the glow of torches and Chinese lanterns hung from the towering monarchs.[102]

Thanks to the railroad, during the first year of Hooper's management nearly nine thousand people visited Big Trees Grove. The following season, the *Santa Cruz Sentinel* declared that owing to the good accommodations provided, visitation would likely double soon.[103] That spring, a *Santa Cruz Courier* correspondent proclaimed that after having "visited the grove a great many times at all seasons of the year, we must say that there is nothing of the same nature in the State that can possibly surpass, if it can equal it, and no tourist or visitor to Santa Cruz County will have seen one of her most delightful attractions until the Big Tree Grove has been visited."[104] Not all were pleased with the improvements; some preferred the original wild character of the landscape. A lady visitor disappointedly described the grove "with its carefully kept grounds, its potted plants, its hotel where you may have high-priced lunch, and its little tables suggestive of lager and pretzels."[105]

Those eager to leave their mark on Big Trees Grove began a practice by the 1870s that lasted well into the early twentieth century. Visitors tacked personal calling cards and notes on the soft bark of the largest trees. The monarch known today as the Giant was the first focus of this attention and for years wore a "great corset of cards."[106] Many of the trees were *thickly covered with bits of paper which from a distance look as if they had fluttered about on trembling wing and lit upon it, drawn by some attraction. Upon nearer view they are cards, scraps of waste paper, backs of old envelopes, fastened with nails, spikes, pins, anything to keep them in place. Alas! The irrepressible, pompous tourist has been here by the hundred, and here he leaves his record.[107]*

Such notes were not only attached to a tree's bark, but in the case of the Fremont Tree, they were either tacked directly to the fire-scarred interior or placed on a shelf nailed across from the entrance. While recording plant data in his 1910 field book, naturalist Willis Linn Jepson also noted this unique preoccupation of grove visitors:

The people who came to visit the grove of Big Redwood trees at Felton struck us by their actions in one particular. They came in…little parties of 2 to 10 and went straight to [certain] trees and began reading the visitors cards tacked on the tree by the thousands,—cards of tailors at Santa Cruz, barbers at San Jose, shop-keepers from San Francisco and members of the Order of the Screaming Eagle from Kansas etc.[108]

This tradition would come under heavy criticism from the grove's most distinguished visitor.

The Fremont Tree was the premier attraction for visitors. One commentator showed little regard for the tree's history or for Frémont, stating that the Fremont Tree was "hollow and rotten (like its namesake) at the heart."[109] Most visitors saw Frémont as an American hero, and the management of Big Trees Grove agreed. Many early photographs show American flags draped across the tree's entrance, making the Fremont Tree practically a shrine to the explorer. Sometimes it was called the "House-tree" due to the large fire-carved hollow at its base that was often compared to a room. The cavity measures approximately twelve by fifteen feet with a ceiling about twenty-six feet high.[110] Many stories claimed the tree was occupied in the past by runaway sailors, an outlaw, tannery workers, a shoe cobbler and even a lumberman and his wife with a newborn child. One story claimed the hollow was inhabited as early as 1835.[111]

Previous to the Mexican war, when local commotions were prevalent, persons finding concealment necessary resorted to these trees as a refuge. Buried among the wild and somber recesses of mountain forests, remote

A dapper gentleman poses at the base of the Giant, circa 1880s. *Courtesy of Frank Perry.*

from habitations and difficult to find, these trees, many of which are hollow, ofttimes afforded the weary refugee a haven.[112]

The earliest known account of trying to fit a large group of people within the Fremont Tree's hollow came from an article titled "Curiosities of Santa Cruz" in the November 8, 1862 issue of the *Santa Cruz Weekly Sentinel*. The claim was of thirty people standing inside at one time. That same year, artist Edward Vischer noted that the only source of light came from the entrance, implying no window had yet been cut through the bark.[113] At some point, an axman stood on the outside of the tree and hacked away, creating at least one window and a stovepipe hole. The window opening was supposedly large enough for a ten-year-old boy to climb through.[114] In

A group of visitors gathered at the Fremont Tree, circa 1880s. *Special Collections, University Library, University of California–Santa Cruz (Santa Cruz Historical Photographs Collection).*

Girls at the Fremont Tree entrance taken by Martin Reese, circa 1887. *Special Collections, University Library, University of California–Santa Cruz (Santa Cruz Historical Photographs Collection).*

her 1882 *Sketches of an American Tour*, Lady Duffus Hardy noted that one window had a glass pane.[115] Throughout the nineteenth century, many visitor accounts mentioned the presence of two windows. By 1889, another visitor noted that "one of the openings has been closed entirely, and the others are becoming grown over."[116]

The generally mild climate of the Santa Cruz region was especially attractive to visitors and ensured a long tourist season at Big Trees Grove. Hooper touted that "the temperature at the Grove is adapted to evening parties, as no fogs prevail there during the entire Summer."[117] This is a strange boast to those familiar with the often-damp summer evenings in the redwood forest. Winters in the grove, though, always have the potential to be quite harrowing. During the winter of 1877–78, Hooper had to leave the grove four times on account of falling trees. During one particularly violent windstorm, Hooper and his family spent a night within the shelter of the Fremont Tree. During the storm, "the trees groaned and lashed one another, falling here and there, their tops, as they swayed about, looking like an angry sea, and the sound of their fall was like unto the explosion of a hundred cannon."[118] The trees in the grove that are most often felled by strong winds are the shallow-rooted Douglas fir. Though the redwoods also have a somewhat shallow root system, those roots also extend outward a couple of hundred feet and intertwine with the roots of neighboring redwoods, thereby making them more resistant to toppling from strong winds. The greatest threat during a storm was, and still is, the falling of large redwood limbs.

Along with growing popularity came growing problems. The grove was not immune to the vices of the times. The 1881 picnic excursion of the Unity Society of San Jose brought three hundred attendees, who included

> *two hundred hoodlums….Many of them were drunk….[S]traightway they made for the bar, and when the more drunken ones were refused liquor one of the toughest threatened to knock Major Hooper down. Not a bottle would the Major allow filled over the bar. A gang of rowdies sat down to the dinner-table, and after eating to their fill eight of them failed to pay their bills, four of the number jumping the fence and running into the woods. By request the bar was closed for an hour….[Then] the fighting commenced in earnest. It was curse, jaw, knock-down and haul off, the policemen who had accompanied this delectable crowd having all they could do.*[119]

Another recurring issue that Hooper faced was gambling. Numerous times he ran gamblers out of the grove, complaining that tourists did not come to the Big Trees "to be fleeced by a horde of backlegs...and that he was armed and ready to defend his life and property" if need be.[120] Though Hooper kept the Big Trees in "apple-pie order"[121] and he and his wife were said to be "kind to the traveling Bohemian,"[122] he was unable to make a profit and left in bankruptcy in 1881. His total effects amounted to only $148.25, but his indebtedness largely exceeded that amount.[123]

Chapter 5

UNDER THE MOUNTAINS AND THROUGH THE WOODS

The Switzerland of America!
—*South Pacific Coast Railroad advertisement, circa 1880s*

An 1880s railroad advertisement proudly compared the Santa Cruz Mountains to the Alps, dubbing the region "the Switzerland of America!"[124] Despite the descriptive exaggeration, the Santa Cruz Mountains did serve as a formidable obstacle to rail access. For many years, the people of Santa Cruz were anxious for a shorter rail connection to the San Francisco Bay Area, especially for exporting their valuable lumber and lime resources.

In the late 1870s, the challenge of constructing a shorter rail route via the Santa Cruz Mountains was taken up by the South Pacific Coast Railroad (SPCRR). The new railway ran from the Municipal Port of Oakland and traveled down the East Bay through San Jose. Getting to Santa Cruz meant having to go under portions of the daunting Santa Cruz Mountains. Construction of the route was a tremendous engineering feat. Traversing the Santa Cruz Mountains required the building of six tunnels. As with most railroad construction in the West, the Chinese played a major role. The construction of the SPCRR was no different, with a work crew that was over 90 percent Chinese.

Tunneling was an arduous undertaking. Tunnel No. 3, near the town of Wrights, measured nearly a mile and a quarter, making it the second-longest railroad tunnel in California and taking a train a full six minutes to pass

Advertisement for the South Pacific Coast Railroad (SPCRR), circa 1880s. *Courtesy of the Santa Cruz Museum of Art and History.*

through. Cutting the tunnel took twenty-seven months to complete. It was also extremely dangerous work. On November 17, 1879, Tunnel No. 3 was the scene of tragedy. A fire ignited a pocket of highly flammable methane gas, causing an explosion that "shook the mountains from base to summit," killing thirty-two Chinese workers.[125]

Growing hostility toward Chinese laborers eventually culminated in the Chinese Exclusion Acts in the 1880s, which severely limited immigration from China until the mid-twentieth century. The anti-Chinese sentiment in Santa Cruz, led by *Santa Cruz Sentinel* editor Duncan McPherson and local businessman and minister Elihu Anthony, was particularly virulent. On at least one occasion, ugly racial politics entered the Big Trees. In 1878, the grove hosted the Workingmen's Club picnic. Locals, including workers from Henry Cowell's IXL Lime Works, arrived on wagons bearing mottoes proclaiming, "The Chinese must go." Interestingly, Cowell went against local consensus and continued to hire Chinese workers.[126] His employment of the Chinese and newly arrived immigrants likely allowed him to pay lower wages than his competitors.

A platform was erected beneath the redwoods where the featured speaker railed against monopolies and decried corporations run by a "privileged class of robbers, land-grabbers, mining and railroad sharps and stock gamblers" and advocated for workers' rights and fair taxation. But his speech also reflected the rising tide of hostility toward the Chinese. The speaker proclaimed that "50,000 of them are now in San Francisco, and are the direct cause of hoodlumism....Help us to drive them out and we will help you regulate your taxation and monopolies."[127] A rare positive view of the Chinese was voiced in the grove the following year when a visiting railroad employee was charmed by a

> *Chinaman who keeps a store at the entrance of the ground and supplies railroad hands....* [He] *invited us to his domicile and, with politeness that would shame many a white man, sat before us the refreshments much needed at that time, and on my requesting his name, he wrote, in a clear, bold hand, in English, "Quong Long Sing." This is not the first time I have experienced the hospitality of Americanized Chinamen.*[128]

At first, the Welch family did not welcome the new rail line, even commencing a suit for damages against the railroad in 1879 because the route would cut through the heart of the grove.[129] The resort's manager took a different view. After completion of the tracks across the San Lorenzo River,

George Colegrove and a railroad construction crew were enthusiastically greeted with champagne by Big Trees Grove tenant John Hooper.[130] With the completion of the rail line in 1880, the resort began to greatly benefit from the new route. It was a hit with visitors, with more tourists flocking to Big Trees Grove each season. Ferry steamers conveyed passengers from the landing at the foot of Market Street in San Francisco to Alameda in twenty-five minutes. The trains originally ran at a maximum speed of thirty miles per hour, transporting visitors to Big Trees Grove in record time, a vast improvement over the slower and more trying stagecoach mode of travel.[131] The rail company touted that "passengers can leave San Francisco on Sunday morning early, reach Santa Cruz in four hours, take a surf bath, enjoy a picnic at the grove and return to the city by night."[132] The railroad company also claimed the scenery along its route was the most diversified of any road running out of San Francisco.

First passing through the beautiful town of Alameda, with rows of slender eucalyptus trees on either side, the road crosses an arm of the bay (San Leandro), and runs between San Francisco Bay and the foothills of the Coast Range mountains, over the salt marsh where stacks of salt glisten in the sun "like the tents of an army encamped." This salt is produced in large quantities by the evaporation of sea-water, and is mostly used in the mining regions for the reduction of ores. It is stacked up and remains unsheltered, like the huge piles of grain and straw to be seen on both sides of the road.

At Alvarado the Beet Sugar Mills are located….After twenty-five miles of travel in almost a straight line, passing strawberry, asparagus, tomato, and onion ranches of many acres in extent, the town of Newark, where the Company's workshops are located, is reached. From this point can be obtained a good view of Mount Hamilton, where the Lick Observatory is located.[133]

Dark streaks, about a yard wide, on the ground on either side of the train proved to be prunes drying in the sun on wire frames. There were miles upon miles of them and there seemed to be enough prunes to supply the world.[134]

Leaving San Jose, we pass over a nearly level country of upland to Los Gatos. Here is the "natural home of the grape," and here we enter and begin our ascent of the Santa Cruz Mountains….From the higher peaks San Francisco Bay, fifty miles to the northward can be seen; and toward the south and west, apparently but a few miles away, rolls the Pacific Ocean and Monterey Bay, whilst toward the southeast the mountain range culminates in a high peak, called by the Spaniards Loma Prieta (Dark Mountain)….

The road follows the Los Gatos Creek through solidly-arched tunnels and around graceful curves. The air is fragrant with the odor of ceanothus, manzanita, madrone, yerba santa and mountain laurel (bay tree). The rocky cliffs take all manner of queer forms, resembling pyramids, castles, domes, etc. In one place there is a narrow cleft one hundred feet deep, as though some giant had commenced to split off part of the mountain, and left his work unfinished. The streams as they meander through the canyon, always in sight of the road, are clear as crystal in the summer.

By tunnels we have passed under the summit of this mountain range, and, having reached Glenwood station, we begin to descend. We follow Bean Creek and the Zayante to where they join the San Lorenzo River at Felton. Here is the terminus of a huge flume, down which are floated the products of the forest of the upper San Lorenzo country. Half a mile further down we come to the famous "Big Tree Grove."[135]

In 1887, a Missouri visitor described his group's excitement as they approached the grove:

As our train dashed along through the forest some of our companions cried out to us, "Look, look, see that one! Isn't he a buster! There is Gen. Grant; and look, there is Gen. Fremont!" and we gazed in wonder at these grand old giant trees towering up toward the sky so high that we could not see their tops from the moving train.[136]

The SPCRR boasted its route was forty miles shorter than any other, saving at least two and a half hours' travel time. The company vigorously promoted visiting Big Trees Grove and the nearby campgrounds, advertising no change of cars, no dust and even no mosquitoes. The success of the route helped transform the lumber town of Felton into the "Tourists' and Campers' Paradise."[137]

Chapter 6

PICNICKERS AND PLEASURE SEEKERS

In every great trunk an epic lies,
A psalm in every branch that scales the skies!
—*anonymous*

Just as seasonal campgrounds began to spring up around the town of Felton, the grove itself was in a slight decline. After John Hooper's bankruptcy, the resort was described as desolate with "vacated buildings, open doors, waterless pipes, unswept paths, deserted retreats, empty vials and cold cook-stoves."[138] In 1882, David Metcalf Aldrich took on the challenge of Big Trees Grove. Aldrich, a native of Susquehanna County, Pennsylvania, first came to California as a young man with his family in 1850. He tried his hand at many occupations, including miner and tax collector in the Sierra gold country. By 1870, he had moved to Illinois to try farming, but he returned to California by 1880, eventually settling in Watsonville.[139]

At the outset of Aldrich's tenancy, he and his son began making improvements to Big Trees Road leading from the old Toll House. Big Trees Grove was often visited by camping parties from the San Francisco Bay Area. Nature camping became more popular than ever, and the number of seasonal campgrounds multiplied near the grove, with names like Camp Lolita and Camp Frolic. The latter drew its members from the Frolic Social Club of San Francisco, located in the Western Addition.[140] Sometimes single camping groups numbering up to two hundred people would set up housekeeping in Felton for the entire summer season. One large party in June 1880 sent down three railcar loads of freight in advance of their visit:

> *They have thirty-four white tents…*[with] *a large majority of women and children during the week, but on Saturdays the husbands and fathers come down to spend Sunday with their families in the quiet shades of this most beautiful grove. They spend their time hunting, fishing, bathing, gathering ferns, flowers, etc. and in visiting the different lime-kilns, mills…*[then] *go to Santa Cruz and take a plunge in the ocean and come back on the next train.*[141]

The camping season lasted from March until December and gave the place the air of a military camp.[142]

With the full benefit of rail service from both Santa Cruz and Oakland, Big Trees Grove events during Aldrich's management began to draw larger crowds, and some became annual occurrences. The Bango Club, established in 1876, was a walking group of prominent local businessmen who held annual one- to two-week camps for hundreds of their members and families.[143] The Bangos often competed in wrestling and stone-throwing matches and exhibitions of fancy horseback riding. At an 1885 event, the Bangos were serenaded with minstrel songs by a "colored guitarist" named Albert Logan, otherwise known as Blonde.[144] Logan, born into slavery in Arkansas, came to California sometime after the Civil War with his mother and two brothers. Originally settling in Watsonville, by 1887 Logan and his wife, Mary, had bought a two-story house on South Branciforte Avenue in Santa Cruz. For many years, they operated their home as a boardinghouse that also served as a center for Santa Cruz's growing African American community.[145] In addition to his business, Logan also hired out to cook picnic meals for various groups. Logan was described as "so large that the Big Trees look small in comparison. He is good natured and keeps the 'Bangos' in good spirits and plenty of well-cooked edibles."[146] That meal consisted of about two thousand clams roasted on piles of seaweed and dishes of roast turkey, chicken and baked fish paired with wine and champagne punch.[147]

In addition to pleasant tourist experiences, Big Trees Grove also hosted some darker episodes involving rough crowds. In May 1890, one group of excursionists was composed of men, women and boys under the influence of liquor. The picnic, given by the Dolphin Swimming and Boating Club of San Francisco,

The Bango Club, organized in 1876, was a local men's walking club that held its annual campouts at Big Trees Grove. *Santa Cruz Public Libraries.*

A group makes its way to Big Trees Grove from the nearby Christian retreat Mount Hermon, circa 1910. *Author's personal collection.*

was one of the toughest ever held at the Big Trees. Twenty-seven cars filled with excursionists "pulled up" at the grove, and over fifteen hundred people alighted. Sheriff Jennings stopped four gambling games which had been established among the trees....Fights during the day were frequent, and [Sheriffs] Jennings and Sam Morgan gamely stepped in between combatants, scattering them right and left....[Sheriff Morgan] was determined to arrest the man who had clubbed him, so that when he caught sight of him on the train he made haste to reach him. When he boarded the car a crowd of toughs jumped on him, bearing him to the floor and taking his pistol away. As he was in danger of being badly injured the officer caught the ear of the fellow on top of him between his teeth, causing the fellow to cry for mercy. This gave Morgan a chance to get up, for the crowd stepped back and the tough arose, his ear smarting with pain. Sam now taking out a pair of handcuffs went through the cars, striking right and left on each side of the two cars he passed through. Sam's passage through the cars was strewn with the prostrate forms of bad men, who had the hardihood to tackle the game officer. When Felton was reached the train did not stop. When near Eccles the officer jumped from the train while it was in motion, as he had all the fun he wanted for one day. Luckily he was not injured in jumping from the flying train.[148]

Though Aldrich made improvements to the road and ensured a good water supply, he left in 1885 after four years of a six-year lease, lamenting that visitors were too often prey for "card flippers and dice slingers."[149] The Aldrich family moved to Stockton.

GOD'S FIRST TEMPLES

The new nature tourism of the nineteenth century frequently inspired visitors to describe the scenery they encountered in spiritual terms. The roots of this sprang from both eighteenth-century literary and artistic Romanticism and nineteenth-century Transcendental philosophy of people like Ralph Waldo Emerson and Henry David Thoreau. The Transcendentalist beliefs in self-reliance and the divinity of nature influenced thinkers like John Muir, who felt that mountains, animals and trees were the "terrestrial manifestations of God." This was particularly true in the mammoth redwood forests.[150] A visitor in 1899 felt that *since my first visit to Niagara I have come across nothing in nature which so moved me or brought me so close to Him who wrought this marvelous work, and with moistened eyes I stood in awe and reverence before these monarchs of the wood. And the familiar lines of* [William Cullen] *Bryant's Forest Hymn seemed an appropriate outlet to my surcharged thoughts: "The groves were God's first temple..."*[151]

Another visitor in 1904 gave soaring words to his impressions of the majestic trees.

As one stands within the rich cathedral gloom, cast by the shadows of these massive steeples, the mind reflects upon the dignity and meaning of it all. For these trees are the oldest living things on earth! Their records, which they themselves inscribe from year to year, around their hearts, prove them to be centuries, yea, thousands of years old. How often have they been used as an altar to their Maker, how many human generations have, under their shady branches differently pronounced the name of God, but who recognized [H]*im everywhere in His works, and adored Him in His manifestations. They stood to witness the birth of Christ; they have seen nations rise and fall; they have known races of which we have never learned; they have heard the chanting and prayer of religious creeds innumerable, and in their great, deep and unbreakable silence, keep their secrets well.*[152]

Since spiritual terms and biblical allusions were frequently used to describe the Big Trees, it is little wonder that the naming of one tree in 1884 caused some controversy. On October 4, Big Trees Grove was paid a visit by one of the most famous men of the time, Robert Ingersoll.[153] The name is not as familiar today, but in the nineteenth century, Ingersoll was considered one of our nation's greatest and most controversial orators. As a critic of fundamentalist religion, he was often called the "Great Agnostic." Ingersoll became famous for his lectures on ethics and humanism and may have been heard by more people in his lifetime than any other American. He was in Santa Cruz to give one of his most popular lectures, "The Liberty of Man, Woman and Child," at Bernheim's Music Hall.[154] On the morning of his lecture, Ingersoll made his way to Big Trees Grove for a picnic and to have his photograph taken next to a Big Tree. In the vein of satire, the multi-trunk tree that served as the photo's backdrop became known as Ingersoll's Cathedral. Due to its unique natural attributes, the tree was often cited as the most interesting in the grove, "poised in the sky three hundred feet or

Ingersoll's Cathedral was named for nineteenth-century orator Robert Ingersoll, who was lauded for his lectures on humanism and ethics. *Courtesy of Ross Eric Gibson.*

The YMCA Tree was dedicated in 1887. *Courtesy of the Santa Cruz Museum of Art and History.*

more above the head of the tallest worshiper. It is surrounded at almost regular distances by twelve smaller trees, living columns engirdling a living temple, older than St. Peter's and a brother of the Parthenon."[155] In 1893, the sign bearing Ingersoll's name was torn down from the tree. One observor described the unknown perpetrator as "probably some one who differs from Col. Ingersoll, but has not been able to express himself otherwise."[156]

In 1887, delegates of the San Francisco convention of the Young Men's Christian Association (YMCA) came down to Big Trees Grove for a tree dedication. They selected another multi-trunk tree nearby Ingersoll's Cathedral that they thought was symbolic of their organization.[157] Some of the grove guides evidently got great pleasure in pointing out the two trees to visitors. "'What a pity!' exclaimed a lady of our party when the name of this masterpiece of the forest [Ingersoll's Cathedral] was announced. The guide quickly drew her attention to the Y.M.C.A. group which could not hold a pine-knot to Ingersoll's cathedral, and a merry twinkle in his tell-tale eyes was evidence that he knew it and enjoyed the situation."[158] In 1911, the International Sunday School Association journeyed to Santa Cruz as part of its convention festivities. They also asked permission of the Welch brothers to have a Big Tree dedicated to their organization. A redwood was felt to be an appropriate symbol since the tree's Latin name means "evergreen" or "never dying." The association selected the same redwood that the YMCA had back in 1887, and for the same reason—so it could be a counterpoint to Ingersoll's Cathedral.[159]

Chapter 7

THE COAST REDWOODS VERSUS THE GIANT SEQUOIAS

They seem to understand that they bore the names of the best men, and the grandest heroes America has ever produced, and had made themselves worthy to bear their names by towering far above the common forest trees.
—Jessie Bunn, Jackson [OH] Standard, *March 22, 1888*

In the late nineteenth century, a visit to Big Trees Grove in the Santa Cruz Mountains rivaled and, early on, even surpassed in popularity a visit to their celebrated and more remote cousins, the giant sequoia of the Sierra Nevada. Their dimensions astounded visitors, the coast redwood being the tallest and the giant sequoia being the largest living things on earth.

The redwoods and the giant sequoias were popularized with the telling of their discovery stories, recounting their dimensions in terms of board feet of lumber and reciting the exploits of the famous individuals for whom they were named. Both species were often described in the language of the sublime and picturesque popular at the time, and both were declared "must-see destinations" for a tour of California.[160] Despite not gaining wide public acclaim until the gold rush, the giant sequoias were the first to be recognized as a tourist draw. By 1853, the first sequoia region to be commercialized was the Calaveras Grove located outside Murphys in Calaveras County. The first trickle of tourists to the Mariposa Grove to the south arrived by the late 1850s.[161] Each region was popularized through the lithographs of Edward Vischer. During a visit to Santa Cruz in 1862, the artist said, "The Big Trees of Santa Cruz will bear comparison with the Big Trees of Calaveras."[162]

An estimated seven hundred visitors made it to Yosemite Valley between 1855 and 1864, but only half of them may have reached Mariposa Grove.[163] During the same period, it can be speculated that a few thousand people visited Big Trees Grove. In 1881, the Mariposa Grove became more famous when the Washburn family authorized a passage cut through the base of a living sequoia. The tree that could allow passage of a stagecoach through it became known as the Wawona. Not to be left out, around the same time a similar cut was made into the base of a sequoia in the Calaveras Grove called the Pioneer Tree.[164] Adding to the competition, the proprietors of Big Trees Grove boasted in 1902 of

> a tree, which has a rift in it through which two horses and a surrey can be driven without touching either side, similar to the famous tree in the Calaveras Grove through which a stage coach has been driven, with the exception that the tree in our Big Tree grove has not been trimmed or hewn in any way to increase its aperture.[165]

The tree described may be the Natural Graft Tree, which visitors can still walk through on the Redwood Loop Trail today. Thankfully, one Los Gatos resident's suggestion that same year to cut a hole through the Giant never came to fruition.[166]

With rail service commencing in 1875 and a second rail line from Oakland starting in 1880, visitation at Big Trees Grove continued to increase. By 1887, two passenger trains ran daily to and from San Francisco and three to and from Santa Cruz.[167] A stage line also ran twice a day between Santa Cruz and Boulder Creek.[168] Throughout the 1880s and 1890s, even single event organization picnics at the grove drew one to more than two thousand attendees each. A conservative estimate would place the visitation figure for Big Trees Grove from a couple of hundred thousand to perhaps as high as half a million visitors by the turn of the century. The 1890 *California Guide for Tourists and Settlers* advised potential tourists that for "those whose limit of time will not permit of a trip to the Mariposa or Calaveras Big Trees, a most excellent substitute may be found within three hours' ride of San Francisco, and on one of the most romantic and interesting routes of travel in the State, viz., the South Pacific Coast Railroad through the Santa Cruz Mountains."[169] As late as 1905, Big Trees Grove was still touted as an easier trip than going to see the giant sequoias of the Sierras. Big Trees Grove "is most convenient and the only one that can be reached without a long stage ride. A narrow-gauge railroad runs trains to it every hour in about thirty minutes [from Santa Cruz]….Calaveras grove, Tuolumne, Mariposa, General Grant Park and the Sequoia Park are all reached by stage rides of from forty to seventy-five miles."[170]

Many early visitors believed the great size of the redwoods and the giant sequoias meant that they lived to an equally great age. A common belief was that the largest trees were 5,000 years old. It is now understood that the giant sequoia can reach over 3,000 years. Most coast redwoods live between 500 and 1,500 years, with the oldest reaching just beyond 2,000. Today, the oldest tree in Big Trees Grove is believed to be the Giant, with an age estimated from 1,800 to over 2,000 years. Size, though, does not necessarily equal age, since the width of a tree's annual growth ring is affected by many environmental factors from annual moisture to the available amount of sunlight. The only true way to measure a tree's age is to take either a coring or section to count the rings.

Several pioneering naturalists visited the coast redwoods. In 1872, the Big Trees of the San Lorenzo Valley were investigated by Asa Gray, professor of botany at Harvard University.[171] In 1910, Big Trees Grove welcomed Willis Linn Jepson, author of the seminal works on the flora and trees of California.[172] By far the most well-known naturalist to visit the region was John Muir. During the summer of 1877, John Muir traveled to the Santa Cruz Mountains. Exactly where he traversed the redwood forest is unknown, but in a letter to a friend that September, he wrote that he "had a glorious ramble in the Santa Cruz woods & have found out one very interesting & picturesque fact concerning the growth of this Sequoia. I mean to devote many a long week to its study." Unfortunately, in the letter he didn't specify the nature of that "interesting & picturesque fact." Perhaps the feature of the redwoods that so astounded him was their ability to sprout not only from seeds but also from their roots, particularly after fires or other damage, since Muir titled one of his sketches from this journey "Redwood Near Santa Cruz. Fired and Renewed."[173] The redwoods' second growth sets them apart from most other trees, including Muir's beloved giant sequoia, which are incapable of such regeneration. Often when a parent redwood tree dies and is no longer visible, the new generation of redwoods that sprouted from its roots continues to grow in the form of a circle. The best example in the park of such a family or fairy circle is the group that includes the Fremont Tree. Today, picnic tables are situated where this family's parent tree once stood.

Though a single mature redwood can produce over 100,000 seeds annually, most trees in Big Trees Grove today have sprouted from the roots of parent trees. This begs the question: just how old are the root systems

Left: A post-1906 Southern Pacific Railroad advertisement for Big Trees Grove. *Courtesy of Jim Kliment*.

Below: A group of tourists poses in front of the Giant, circa 1880s. *Courtesy of History San Jose*.

of these monarchs of the forest? Answers may come in the near future. In 2019, the genome of the coast redwood was successfully sequenced by scientists from the University of California–Davis and Johns Hopkins University in cooperation with the Save the Redwoods League. This new research reveals the complexity of the coast redwoods. Human beings have three billion "base pairs" of DNA. The giant sequoia has eight billion, while the coast redwood possesses an astounding twenty-seven billion.[174] Though much of this difference likely springs from genetic repetition, redwood scientists still have much work ahead of them to unravel the mysteries of the remarkable redwood.

What's in a Name?

Both the coast redwood (*Sequoia sempervirens*) and the giant sequoia (*Sequoiadendron giganteum*) share the genus name *Sequoia*, which was bestowed on them by Steven Endlicher, a German botanist, in 1847. The name derives from the Cherokee Indian Sequoyah, who created an alphabet for his people in 1821. Since Endlicher was both a botanist and linguist, he was well acquainted with and appreciative of Sequoyah's accomplishment and felt it was a fitting appellation for the monarchs of the forest.[175]

The individual naming of the Big Trees began virtually from the moment of their discovery by Americans. This was the case for both the redwoods and giant sequoias. The first widely known name applied to a coast redwood, of course, was Fremont's Tree, known today as the Giant. The name was originally bestowed on it by Isaac Graham in honor of that famous explorer's visit to the grove in the spring of 1846. This tallest of the grove's Big Trees was also occasionally known as the San Lorenzo Giant, named after the spectacular canyon in which it stands.[176]

Some of the first names given to both species during the nineteenth century were inspired by the Civil War. In Big Trees Grove and Sequoia and General Grant National Parks, trees were named for Generals Sherman and Grant. These heroic appellations were bestowed on the giant sequoias before they were given to their coast redwood cousins.[177] During John Hooper's tenure at Big Trees Grove, the tradition of naming the most impressive Big Trees began in earnest and would continue well into the early twentieth century. Several trees standing near the General Sherman at Big Trees Grove were known as Sherman's Lieutenants and included Generals Sheridan and

Logan.[178] Perhaps Hooper's Massachusetts roots explain why some of the first trees were named in honor of Union heroes of the Civil War. Naturalist John Muir could not understand how

> *the childish, unsightly, and paltry practice could have arisen, and could continue apparently without objection, of labelling them with the names of cities, states, and persons. I confess I am amazed at the general obliviousness to the disgrace of the thing, even among cultivated persons, and am compelled to believe that the people who come to view them have no real appreciation of their grandeur, but look upon them merely with a Barnum eye as curiosities and "big things."*[179]

Little attention was paid to such sentiments, and the naming of trees at both redwood and giant sequoia groves continued for decades.

Most monarchs in Big Trees Grove were named after notable men. The grove contains a Centennial Group for which each tree among them was named for a Revolutionary War hero, including Washington, Jefferson,

From the 1880s to the 1930s, the highlight of an organization's picnic visit to Big Trees Grove was often a tree dedication. *Courtesy of Frank Perry.*

Redwood Burl
AND ITS USES

A REDWOOD TREE HAVING A GROWTH
OF BURL.

Left: The Giant Burl Tree graces the cover of George Hopkins's redwood novelty brochure. *Courtesy of the San Lorenzo Valley Museum.*

Below: A young girl poses at the Jumbo Tree. A portion of the dance floor can be seen in the background. *Courtesy of Frank Perry.*

Adams, Monroe, Hamilton and Franklin. This family circle, apparently located near the hotel, included what is believed to be the first tree in the grove named after a woman: the Martha Washington.[180] In a nod to California's origin story, along with the Fremont Tree, there was also a corresponding General Castro Tree. Some names were inspired by mythology, such as the Nine Muses and Three Graces. Some trees received names descriptive of a feature they possessed, such as the Giant Burl Tree. Burls are the hard, woody growth usually found at the base of some redwood trees. The swirled grain patterns of burl result from the entwined growth around clusters of dormant buds and are valued by woodworkers for their beauty.[181] Other trees were named for their similarity to animals, as in the case of the Jumbo Tree, presumably named for the large protruding burl resembling the head of an elephant. In the early 1880s, the African elephant named Jumbo was a wildly popular feature of showman P.T. Barnum's circus.[182]

Begun as a way to honor certain individuals, the tradition of naming trees at Big Trees Grove became a way to encourage visitation. By the 1880s, large fraternal, religious and business organizations visited Big Trees Grove as part of their annual meetings or conventions. Many tourist seasons saw multiple tree dedications. In 1913, one visitor commented on the frequency and growing absurdity of the ritual, stating that

> one or two of the largest bore inscriptions,—"Dedicated to the Los Angeles Produce Exchange by the San Francisco Dairy and Fruit Exchange"; and "Dedicated to Reading Commandery No. 42 Knights Templars of Pennsylvania." I pondered these inexplicable labels for some time, and could only conclude that they were examples of the same pitiful ambition that Hamlet observed in a certain kind of players.[183]

To date, the names of one hundred trees have been recorded, with some trees bearing two or more names. Unfortunately, the locations of most of them have been lost to history. See Appendix A.

Chapter 8

THE HEYDAY OF BIG TREES GROVE

The forests of America, however slighted by man,
must have been a great delight to God;
for they were the best he ever planted.
—*John Muir,* The Atlantic Monthly, *August 1897*

In 1885, Joseph Ball began paying thirty-five dollars a month to lease Big Trees Grove.[184] A native of Toronto, Canada, he became a naturalized citizen in Santa Cruz County in 1874. Ball was an experienced, veteran hotel keeper. By 1882, he was the proprietor of several establishments, including the Grand Central Hotel in Felton. Ball was a man of many talents. He often leased Sunset Park at Glenwood for Sunday picnics and directed work improvements for mountain roadways. He was also quite active in local politics, becoming supervisor of San Lorenzo township in 1900.[185]

At Big Trees Grove, Ball quickly added a store, as well as accommodations for up to forty people. He erected two cottages, one containing four rooms and the other six.[186] The hotel renovations also featured a "broad platform adjoining the main building [behind the Fremont Tree]… fitted with tables and seats and covered with an awning beneath which the picnic parties dine."[187] The resort under Ball's management afforded the visitor numerous amusements, such as fishing, hunting, driving, music and dancing, thereby making "this place second to none on the Pacific Coast."[188] Ball also expanded on one type of amenity that proved quite popular. He constructed a barroom that boasted a bar forty feet long with

Above: In 1885, Joseph Ball added onto the hotel, including a dining porch. *Courtesy of the California History Room, California State Library, Sacramento, California.*

Left: Note the calling cards tacked high above on the tree's bark. J.D. Strong, circa 1880s. *Author's personal collection.*

Right to left: The Fremont Tree, the Jumbo Tree, the Arcade (gazebo) and the Three Sisters. *Courtesy of the Santa Cruz Museum of Art and History.*

a choice assortment of cigars and liquors.[189] It is uncertain if the indoor bar was located with the hotel complex or in a separate structure. He also operated an open-air bar for picnickers situated at the base of the Three Sisters, a row of three trees joined at the roots, including a tree whose base was partly hollowed by fire. Placards advertised "Hot Punch," "Tom and Jerry" and "Sacramento Beer."[190] One lady visitor was not pleased with Ball's new additions, declaring that

> *here in the midst of the beautiful and mighty handiwork of God, Satan has one of his little degrading workshops. We had seen these treacherous man-traps scattered along our journey of near five hundred miles, but we did not expect to see one in this secluded place. As we returned to our tent thinking how the snares of Satan are everywhere spread to capture the young, and wondering when the curse of alcohol would disappear, we noticed a very large redwood stump that showed signs of decay. Around this stump stood nine beautiful trees…forming a circular bower of loveliness. And we thought as those green and flourishing trees will bye and bye destroy that stump, so the glorious circle of temperance men and women who are banded together to work for the good of suffering humanity, will eventually destroy the whiskey traffic.[191]*

Despite the lady's objection, business at Ball's barrooms was quite good. But perhaps it was a bit of divine providence that brought on the 1915 storm that felled the fire-scarred Sister, thereby crushing the outdoor bar.[192] From that point forward, the prostrate tree has been affectionately

The original location of Joseph Ball's bar under the Three Sisters. *Special Collections, University Library, University of California–Santa Cruz (Santa Cruz Historical Photographs Collection).*

Ladies serve lunch on the dining porch, circa 1890s. The wife of proprietor Joseph Ball is second from the right. *Courtesy of Ross Eric Gibson.*

The Big Trees Grove hotel and dining porch located behind the card-covered Fremont Tree. *Courtesy of the Santa Cruz Museum of Art and History.*

known as the Fallen Sister. The burned-out base of the broken giant still stands near the Fremont Tree.

Ball's bill of fare was impressive and included four kinds of meat, two kinds of vegetables, two kinds of bread and three kinds of fruit, besides cakes, pies, tea and coffee.[193] All this for fifty cents a meal. Joseph Ball's cooking inspired the poetic in his customers:

> *Joe's barbecued meat is tall to eat—can not be beat, even at the county seat.*[194]

> *Those who to-day partake of Jo Ball's barbecued beef, from pinching hunger will get relief, and only by eating too much will they come to grief.*[195]

Despite receiving frequent praise for the spreads at his special events, Ball's daily fare was sometimes less than stellar. One patron complained about paying "half a dollar to a greedy hotel-keeper for a scrap of cold ham, a cup of very weak coffee and a piece of sickly looking stale cake."[196] As an experienced hotel keeper, Ball was quite a successful rustler of tourists.[197] When the Welch brothers were once offered double the amount for the lease that Ball was paying them, they refused, stating that they would rather close the grove than have anyone except Ball take charge of the place.[198]

PATHS, NOOKS AND RETREATS

Under Ball's management, the reputation of Big Trees Grove reached new heights. Because the grove was the only forest of great trees, redwood or sequoia, penetrated by a railroad, nearly all tourists in California had it on their itinerary.[199] A visit to the grove was not considered complete without seeing and going inside the Fremont Tree. One gentleman described his group's visit to the famed tree in 1888:

> *Several of us were inside the monster, looking over the thousands of cards pinned to its sides, when it was proposed that we ascertain how many could comfortably stand up in the hollow of this tree. Ladies and gentlemen began piling in like bees into a hive, and when we were pretty well squeezed up together, a young fellow who was lucky enough to be entirely encompassed by fair damsels, seemed to enjoy the situation hugely and persistently cried out: "Send more along, we have plenty of room, yet," while the ladies screamed with excitement, on account of the squeeze—whether with delight or vexation, I will not say.*

This particular group fit a total of forty-two people inside and boasted that their ranks were composed of visitors from fifteen states and territories and one Canadian province.[200]

Though the interior dimensions of the Fremont Tree remain unchanged, its appearance over the years has changed. The window and stovepipe holes cut sometime after 1862 were sealed up by almost one hundred years of bark growth. In the early twentieth century, the Fremont Tree was electrified. A single, bare light bulb hung from the ceiling, illuminating the interior, until 1958. Once again, the only source of light comes from the entrance. That entrance has also altered. Today, adult visitors must bend over or crawl on their knees to gain entrance. Throughout the nineteenth century, visitors easily walked into the tree's hollow. The opening has gradually narrowed as the bark strives to heal the fire scar. Perhaps within fifty or one hundred years, the Fremont Tree will completely seal up and bring an end to a longtime Big Trees Grove tradition.

The sequestered bypaths and nooks were ideal spots for romance, "where, in the sweet seclusion the wild woods grant, wanders many a happy pair."[201] Nearly every day one came across a seated couple, "he with his arms about her slender waist; she tracing erratic lines on the smooth sand with his cane. It's the old, old story, told in the centuries gone beneath these very trees."[202] In

Mother and daughter sit at the base of the Giant. Martin Reese, circa 1880s. *Courtesy of the Santa Cruz Museum of Art and History.*

Tourists stroll along the San Lorenzo River. *Special Collections, University Library, University of California–Santa Cruz (Santa Cruz Historical Photographs Collection).*

This image circa 1910 shows how growth of the Fremont Tree's bark over the past century has narrowed its entrance. *Courtesy of Frank Perry.*

1886, Adolphus Busch, founder of Anheuser-Busch Brewing, was traveling in California in celebration of his silver wedding anniversary.[203] In March, the Busch party drove by carriage from Santa Cruz to Big Trees Grove. They were delighted with the scenery along the road, saying they had seen nothing to equal it in all their travels. An incident that added to the pleasure of the trip of at least two of the party came when Baron Gerhard Eber, of Germany, proposed to Miss Lottie Beneke, of Chicago, under the branches of Ingersoll's Cathedral.[204]

Local writer Josephine Clifford McCrackin amusingly recalled watching tourists arrive at the grove "with their heads thrown back, mouth wide open, eyes bulging out, and frozen stiff in an attitude of wonderment. The fact is that it is difficult to see the top of some of the trees without dislocating your neck."[205] One of the most iconic images of the period was the tourist or group of tourists in the process of measuring the monarchs of the forest. Tourists came equipped with either a tape measure or a ball of twine, and their most frequent target was the largest tree in the grove, the Giant.

It is amusing to see the incredulous tourist, who strongly suspects that he has been listening to or reading a "California yarn," as he approaches this wonderful group, tape measure in hand, determined that there shall be "no foolishness" about the measurements he takes. He measures, he stands afar off and tries to look at the top, he paces around its base, he

Above: In 1906, a party of ladies in their summer white frocks pose with a gentleman before the Giant. *Author's personal collection.*

Opposite, top: Ladies in their best 1880s finery take a brief rest at the Arcade. *Digital image courtesy of the Getty's Open Content Program, J. Paul Getty Museum, Los Angeles.*

Opposite, bottom: A large group of families poses under the Giant, circa 1880s. *Courtesy of the Glass family.*

disposes the members of his party, if there be enough of them, in such a way that, with arms outstretched and finger tips just touching, they embrace the huge circumference and finds that it takes 18 or 19 well-grown human beings to encircle it, then he brings out his tape measure again, and—at last—he believes.[206]

Being the most admired tree in the forest was no protection for the Giant. By 1892, a picket fence was erected to protect it from eastern excursionists who cut large chunks of bark as souvenirs.[207] As further protection, signs were posted and a strip of barbed wire was added between the top posts. Today, split-rail fences protect many of the Big Trees. The redwood's fibrous bark can be over a foot thick and serves as the trees' best protection from fire and insects. The soft bark can easily be damaged if climbed on; therefore, climbing on the roots or trunks of the Big Trees is strictly prohibited.

Big Trees Grove welcomed several very distinguished and wealthy visitors, including Cornelius Vanderbilt III, Crown Prince Vajiravudh of Siam, American orator and politician William Jennings Bryan and co-founder of the *San Francisco Chronicle*[208] M.H. DeYoung.[209] Some came in their own

A fence erected around the Giant prevented visitors from taking souvenirs. *Special Collections, University Library, University of California–Santa Cruz (Santa Cruz Historical Photographs Collection).*

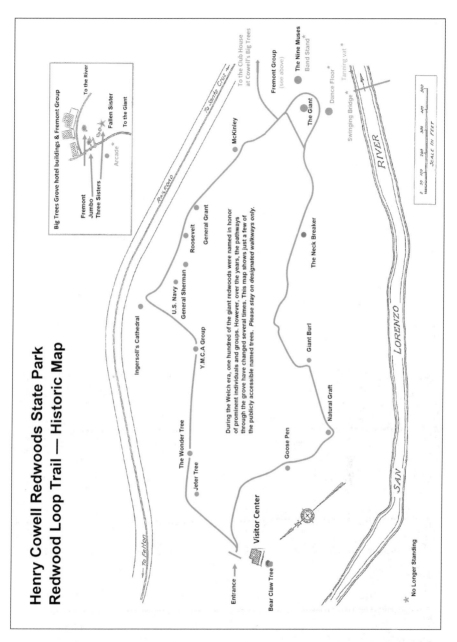

This version of the Redwood Loop Trail map is based on the 1932 Santa Cruz County Big Trees Park brochure. It was revised by Steven Ellmore with input from the author.

"high-toned trains," such as famed oil millionaire John D. Rockefeller. The brief but typical 1903 visit of his party to the Giant was recorded by railroad man George Colegrove:

> *There was one big tree, the largest one in the grove, that had a picket fence around it, about as high as a man's chest. Old John and his son walked around carefully and looked at this tree. There was a sign on this tree that it was sixty feet around in the biggest place. He said to his son, "John, do you think that tree is as big as that?"*
>
> *"Well I guess it is or they wouldn't put that sign on it."*
>
> *"I don't know. I kind of doubt it."*
>
> *I didn't want them to go away thinking it was a mistake, so I got a cotton string and climbed over this picket fence and stuck it on the bark of the tree. I pulled it around the biggest part. I told them to measure it, so they did. They decided it was right. They had found one thing in California that came up to what it was represented.*[210]

Interestingly, the Giant is now shorter than when the resort's early tourists viewed it. At some point, a storm reportedly broke off the tree's top, taking off at least 25 feet. Several accounts claimed up to 70 feet was lost.[211] An item in the *Santa Cruz Daily Surf* gave the Giant's original height as 365 feet and believed the earthquake of 1886 caused the loss of height.[212] Despite conflicting claims, most observers during the late nineteenth century estimated the height at about 306 feet. Whichever the cause or the amount lost, today the Giant's height (just over 275 feet) is about the same as when Frémont first measured it back in 1846.

THE PATHFINDER RETURNS

By the 1870s, the fame and fortunes of John Charles Frémont were in decline. To meet mounting debts incurred while defending his property rights against gold seekers, he reluctantly sold his beloved Mariposa Ranch. Then followed a series of bad investments, including a failed transcontinental railroad scheme. In 1878, the Frémonts were forced to sell all their worldly goods in their New York home. With the help of friends, the family was able to save just two items: a portrait of Mrs. Frémont and a bust of her beloved father, Senator Benton.[213] In 1887, friends came to the rescue once again by helping

In 1888, Big Trees Grove hosted a commemoration of Frémont's earlier California exploits. *Special Collections, University Library, University of California–Santa Cruz (Santa Cruz Historical Photographs Collection).*

the family finance a move to Inglewood, California. Frémont's health and outlook appeared to benefit from the healthier climate. Soon, the Pathfinder began to receive invitations to attend community events in the state that still considered him its hero.

In 1888, the Frémonts agreed to attend a floral fair in San Jose. The trip included a reunion at Big Trees Grove commemorating Frémont's earlier California exploits.[214] On the morning of May 4, Frémont, accompanied by his wife, Jessie, and daughter Elizabeth (also known as Lily) and a few San Jose friends, made their way to Santa Cruz.[215] They were greeted enthusiastically upon arrival at Big Trees Grove. Though now white-haired, Frémont was described as "hale and hearty" with a clear eye, swarthy complexion and "spirit buoyant and his step elastic."[216] Among the reception committee were locals John Daubenbiss and Alfred Baldwin, who both served under Frémont in the Mexican War.[217] After brief introductions, the party was escorted to the Fremont Tree, where photographs were taken of the family.[218] Frémont reminisced about his adventures in 1846 and the several weeks his expedition camped in a clearing near the Big Trees.[219] Supposedly as Frémont stood in front of his namesake tree, a member of the crowd asked the old explorer if a long-told story was true. Back in 1846, did he really sleep in the tree's hollow? Perhaps a trait acquired as a politician to never disappoint the crowd, Frémont reportedly replied in diplomatic fashion, "That's a good story, let it stand."

The Frémonts were next escorted to the Giant, where "sixteen members of the party encircled that immense tree, joining hands; then swinging free from it they formed in a circle apart on the cleared ground, showing

93

Jessie Benton Frémont (with flowers) sits next to her husband and daughter. *Special Collections, University Library, University of California–Santa Cruz (Santa Cruz Historical Photographs Collection).*

the immense growth of this gigantic tree, and thus were photographed by McKean and Reese."[220] The photograph shows Frémont in his bowler hat facing the camera as he held hands with his wife and daughter. The next stop was a luncheon prepared by Big Trees Grove proprietor Joseph Ball. Mayor Gustavus Bowman began the proceedings by toasting Frémont as "our distinguished visitor, the Pathfinder of the Golden West." In response, Frémont acknowledged the compliment and thanked the crowd for their hearty welcome. The old explorer then recalled when the U.S. flag was first

> *unfurled at Monterey, to remain our banner forever....The thrilling experiences and the vicissitudes of those days resulting in adding this great territory to the domain of the United States, made that flag, the emblem of our country, doubly dear to me. Its stars seemed as pure and fixed as the stars in the sky above it, and from that time to the present it represents to me more than ever before the imperishable principles of our government, justice, equality and liberty. To you all, Mr. Speaker, your Honorable Mayor, to you my old comrades in arms, the veterans of the Mexican war, and the Grand Army of the Republic, I desire to again express my sincere thanks for this welcome.*

John Charles Frémont with his namesake tree. Note the calling cards tacked on the interior of the tree. *Courtesy of Frank Perry.*

The Frémonts were among sixteen people on May 4, 1888, who encircled the Giant and then regrouped for a photograph. *Courtesy of the University of Southern California.*

The general closed his remarks amid a burst of applause from the assembled guests. When the train whistle blew, the party hurriedly made their way to the cars, "and in a moment General John C. Fremont and the trees he visited forty-two years ago, then a howling wilderness, the home of bears, were separated by space and steam."[221] As Frémont entered the car, the crowd gave him three rousing cheers.[222]

Before departing, Frémont accepted an invitation from the Santa Cruz Parlor of the Native Sons of the Golden West to be their guest the following September at the California Admission Day celebration. Though that visit never materialized, the parlor's exhibit remained centered on Frémont. The *Santa Cruz Sentinel* described the Admission Day decorations, including a "facsimile of the Big Tree Gen. Fremont, which majestically towers to the ceiling of the Pavilion at the entrance."[223] The absence of the Pathfinder from this tableau re-creating his earlier visit surely disappointed the crowd.

Also in attendance during Frémont's May visit was noted caricaturist and political cartoonist Thomas Nast. Upon departing town, Nast declared the grove grand, adding "that the State ought to own the Big Tree grove and turn it into a public park."[224]

THE RAILROAD PICNIC

In 1887, the South Pacific Coast Railroad route was purchased by Southern Pacific. Little changed in the day-to-day operations of the rail line until the San Francisco earthquake, when subsequent repairs included converting the track to standard gauge. In 1911, Big Tree Station was given a bit more formal appearance with construction of a small ticket booth along the tracks.

In 1889, Joseph Ball was appointed agent for Big Tree Station and soon hosted the grove's largest gathering ever.[225] The picnic of Southern Pacific Railroad employees and their families drew an estimated four thousand partiers who came in

thirty-nine coaches in all, each one more than filled with men, women, children, lunch baskets, babies, young men and maidens—more lunch baskets—boys, girls—lunch baskets—and infants. As fast as the people arrived, they were made welcome by Mr. Ball, the lessee of the grove, and for a time the lunch tables were fully occupied by the happy picnickers. Then, in groups of ten or a dozen, the whole number visited every part of the grove, encircling the "Giant," "General Grant," "Sherman" and

Above: A large tourist group poses beneath the Giant, circa 1880s. *Special Collections, University Library, University of California–Santa Cruz (Santa Cruz Historical Photographs Collection).*

Left: The ticket booth of Big Tree Station was built by Southern Pacific Railroad in 1911. *Courtesy of the Santa Cruz Museum of Art and History.*

Ladies stand at the entrance to the Fremont Tree, circa 1890s. *Courtesy of California State Parks.*

other notable trees. The sequestered by-paths in the grove were occupied by newly-married people, spooney couples and flirting pairs, who, in the sweet seclusion that the wild woods grant, enjoyed themselves immensely.[226]

After a series of foot races, the large crowd proceeded to the dance floor, where the forty-piece Second Artillery Band entertained the crowd "with waltzes, round dances, the schottische, polka, and Spanish dances."[227] With so many in attendance, the dance floor had to be extended twenty-four feet. The ladies present never missed a dance, considering the ratio was four ladies to one gentleman. Officers of the San Francisco police force accompanied the crowd down to Big Trees Grove to prevent pickpockets from interfering with the picnickers. When the first train arrived, "three Eastern crooks established a 'thimble rig' game on a hill near the grounds, and succeeded in relieving one 'seeker after wealth' of $250." Officers quickly stopped the game and sent the crooks back to the city by the first train.[228]

Little Ben at the Big Trees

In preparation for his 1891 visit to California, President Benjamin Harrison was initially not planning to visit Santa Cruz. That changed when an advisor suggested that a visit to the resort town would allow for the president to visit the famed Big Trees Grove. Harrison immediately ordered his itinerary changed.[229] Members of the party included Postmaster General John Wanamaker and Senators Leland Stanford and Charles Felton.[230] Upon arrival at Big Trees Grove on May 1, the presidential party was met by a group of Felton schoolteachers and pupils who greeted the distinguished visitors with cheers, patriotic songs and baskets of flowers.

> *The President and Mrs. Harrison and twenty-five others of the party entered the hollow trunk of the Fremont tree, and thirteen joined hands to encircle the Giant. Postmaster-General Wanamaker carried away the string measures of the biggest tree, and was the most enthusiastic member of the party.*[231]

One reporter had no doubt that the president saw "nowhere upon his route, anything that gave him so much pleasure" as Big Trees Grove.[232] Joseph Ball anticipated getting a photograph of the president during his visit, and in that hope, he invited photographer Martin A. Reese to the event. Ball's request was passed on to the president but refused. Since Harrison viewed his visit to the grove as personal, he demanded that no photographs be taken of him. The president's wishes were respected. It was said that even if a photographer desired to take a photograph of the president, he would have a difficult time since the diminutive Harrison kept almost continually on the move.[233]

Chapter 9

THE SLOW DECLINE

The generations come and go, but these great trees remain. They stood there long before man peopled this western coast; they will remain there long after we who speculate upon their growth have passed away.
—San Francisco Chronicle, *June 9, 1889*

Losing out on publicity from President Harrison's 1891 visit was quite disappointing to Joseph Ball. A commentator that year noted that attendance at Big Trees Grove had fallen off. The description of the grove as a "howling wilderness" appears to have been exaggerated, but by the 1890s, the attraction of Big Trees Grove was changing. Ball complained that eastern excursionists stopped in the grove for only ten or fifteen minutes. He preferred the visitors who camped out in the grove since that afforded him more opportunity for making money off them.[234]

Many locals felt improvements were needed. Ball was willing to implement them, but the barrier appeared to be the owners, the Welch family. A common lament went as follows: "We may fear that the same dead-and-alive condition will continue for another third of a century, unless the property changes hands, for which a supplicant people will continue to ever pray."[235] Herman Welch claimed his family paid sixty dollars a month in taxes and had to keep three men employed to maintain a constant watch against visitors taking strips of bark and branches out of the grove as souvenirs.[236] Contrary to ideal preservation, apparently the Welch family and their managers did not

Left: A group of tourists pause on the swinging bridge over the San Lorenzo River, circa 1900. *Courtesy of the Santa Cruz Museum of Art and History.*

Below: Visitors pose at the Giant, circa 1880s. Note the dance floor (*right*) and the bandstand (*left*). *Brigham Young University, C.R. Savage Collection.*

object to removing pieces of redwood as souvenirs. Rather, they objected to not being compensated for it. In the 1891 guide *Practical Hints for Tourists*, potential visitors were advised that "in exchange for a dime you will get a piece of red wood quite heavy enough for your satchel, or a piece of the bark much too clumsy for your coat pocket."[237]

Many local newspaper editorials suggested that the solution to these woes was the purchase of Big Trees Grove by the railroad, which many hoped would lead to the construction of a grand hotel on the site. The

Welch family refused all such calls to sell out. Their solution was to begin charging an admission fee. In the spring of 1891, Ball built a fourteen-foot-high fence at the entrance. The change was not received well by the people of Santa Cruz.

> *Everybody will be sorry to learn that the Big Trees near Felton are being enclosed by a hideous board fence....We also hear that ten-cents to be charged for a sight of those monarchs of the forest. Some lovers of the beautiful...believe that such majestic monuments of nature's skill as these grand old trees ought to remain free and open, an inspiration to all.*[238]

Though Ball did not want to, he felt compelled to charge an admission fee, as he was "not entirely running the grove for glory." During his first six years of tenancy, Ball expended about $3,000 for improvements.[239] Picnic parties continued to be a regular source of income. At the turn of the century, the grove's moonlight dances remained popular, with some attracting up to five railroad carloads of people for a single event.[240] A continuing draw for out-of-town tourists was the excellent fishing in the San Lorenzo River, considered one of the best steelhead trout and coho salmon regions in Central California.

Despite Ball's management talents, the grove proved to be a hard proposition.

> *The grove pays small rent. Hooper was long in charge of the grove, and he made not a dollar, and left in debt. Aldrich made not a red, and Jo Ball, the present lessee, by hard work of self and wife, has barely made a living. No man has made any clear money out of the Big Trees.*[241]

By the spring of 1900, one commentator described Big Trees Grove as "no longer a popular resort, but a two-bit admission show, patronized almost exclusively by people of the East."[242] Despite the entrance fee being raised to twenty-five cents by 1897, Ball suffered the same fate as his predecessors and left the grove in 1901. The sudden, unexpected death of his wife, Annie, that year likely also contributed to his decision to leave.[243]

THE WELCH FAMILY

After 1900, the Welch brothers began taking a greater role in daily management of the grove. They faced more frequent criticism of their management decisions from all sides: community members, neighboring resorts and the public. *Sentinel* editor Duncan McPherson described the Welch brothers as

> *disagreeable men, and it is a great misfortune to this community that they are the owners of the property....* [They] *have never spent a dollar in the improvement of the property that we know of. The buildings thereon are a lot of tumble-down shanties, presumably erected by tenants, out of whom was exacted every dollar of rent the Grove receipts would bear.* [244]

Perhaps in response to such criticisms, the Welch family incorporated the Big Trees Land and Development Company in 1902. [245] Change came once again in 1905 when family matriarch Anna Welch passed away at the age of eighty. She was described as "one of the few owners of magnificent redwood forests who preferred to protect, rather than cut them down, and her property near Santa Cruz has in consequence been for many years one of the show places of the State." [246] Anna was a true pioneer. She was among a group of New Englanders who arrived in gold rush California in 1849. They traveled via the difficult Isthmus of Panama passage, which required most to walk the tortuous land route or, in the case of female travelers, ride on burros. With the death of her husband in 1875, Anna faced many responsibilities. Suddenly a widow with five children, she maintained a home in San Francisco and 350 acres of land in the Santa Cruz Mountains. Her first order of business was to figure out what to do with the picnic ground. It was Anna who entered into a lease agreement with John Hooper to manage the grove, which set it on the path to becoming one of California's most popular resorts. Anna was also a staunch defender of her property. With the construction of the South Pacific Coast Railroad in 1879, she demanded $5,000 for a right-of-way through her grove, but the railroad refused. In defense of her property rights, Anna filed suit, claiming damages. In the end, she was awarded $1,100, and the railway proceeded to build through the heart of the grove. [247] One story claims that to best protect the trees, Anna recalled her eldest son, Joseph, from his legal studies at the University of California to oversee the rail line clearances. This move ensured that the fewest number of Big Trees would be harmed. Her concern for the health of the grove led to this section of rail line having the tightest clearances of any in the United States.[248] Just as the railroad was coming to completion, Anna suffered yet another blow with the death of her ailing sixteen-year-old son, I. Douglas, in June 1879 of dropsy of the heart.

At her death, Anna's estate, valued at about $20,000 (today amounting to a half million dollars), was passed to her four remaining children, Joseph Jr., Herman, Isabella and Stanly.[249] Daily management of Big Trees Grove fell to the sons, who were often criticized for not expending enough funds to improve the grove's accommodations. Joseph Jr., a lawyer, spent most of his time in Southern California. Most on-site management decisions appeared to fall to Stanly and Herman.[250] The success of the Welch management style can best be understood by a memorable scene played out one day in 1910 when the Knights of Pythias were upset over the grove's gate fee. Over two thousand Knights were about to enter the grove but were surprised when faced with the twenty-five-cent fee per person. Disgusted by the high fee, the two thousand Knights present were bent on showing their disapproval.

Someone found a pair of discarded pantaloons and shirt. These were stuffed with excelsior and legended, "Proprietor of Big Trees; Died of Smallpox." This was hung for a time from a ladder on the music stand. Then an old trunk was secured, and the stuffed figure encoffined. A procession was formed with the Pythians' own brass band at the head and it marched with solemn dirge up to the gateway and around the outer grove, and down

The Fremont Group picnic area. *Santa Cruz, Grove of Big Trees*, circa 1870–1900. Photo by William Henry Jackson. *History Colorado. Accession number 86.200.1281.*

Above: A family poses under a Big Tree, circa 1910. *Author's personal collection.*

Left: Gentlemen pose before the Giant, circa 1900. The man with the megaphone may be serving as a guide. *Courtesy of Ross Eric Gibson.*

to "the island" on the creek. Here the mock funeral came to an end by the burning of the body and the impromptu coffin, the band playing as a preliminary, "Nearer, My God, to Thee," and later, as the smoke rose heavenward, "There Will Be a Hot Time in the Old Town Tonight." The incident seemed to give the excursionists an opportunity to vent their feelings and that was really all that it accomplished.[251]

Frustrations with the Welch management of the grove continued to grow.

GUARDIANS OF THE GATE

Often, upon arrival many visitors were surprised to find Big Trees Grove fronted with a fence and guarded by a guide with outstretched hand awaiting payment of two bits apiece.[252] After passing through the gateway, a guide dressed in rubber boots, cap and coat[253] would take visitors on a ten-minute stroll about the grove, stopping to discourse on each named tree's height, diameter, circumference, age and "the peculiarities of growth, many of which are due to fires in past ages."[254] In addition to recounting the dimensions of each tree, guides also entertained visitors with the exploits, true or not, of early pioneers like Isaac Graham and, of course, John Charles Frémont's famous 1846 expedition. One visitor noted that his "voluble guide would have been talking to this day if the party would have stood to listen to him. Each of the Big Trees had a history which had been wound up in him and had to come forth from him at a certain gait and to a certain amount before he could be induced to move on."[255]

It's uncertain how many guides were employed at the grove over the years, but the names of a few are known. An August 16, 1920 obituary in the *Santa Cruz Evening News* stated that W.H. Orchard served as a Big Trees Grove guide for twenty years and "endeared himself to thousands of Californians and visitors from all over the country by his kindly humor and genial disposition." In 1929, Harley Kelly was also remembered as a longtime grove guide.[256] In 1907, Kelly purchased the saloon at the Toll House located near the entrance road to the grove.[257] He was most noted for his expertise at furnishing redwood burl for the making of curios and jewelry.[258] In the summer of 1909, UC Berkley law student Will Leslie served as a grove guide. He was described as "courteous to the curious and patient with the old....He tells the same story, many times, yet he never seems to be tired of his subject, telling of the early history in a conscientious, earnest way that wins the hearts of all those who hear him."[259]

Perhaps the best known and most beloved Big Trees Grove guide was Harry Staley. Born in San Francisco in 1873, Staley arrived in Felton around 1924 and soon became manager of Big Trees Grove for the Welch family. Once the grove became a county park, he continued serving as a guide.[260] Staley escorted countless visitors through the grove and received letters of commendation from dignitaries all over the world. In 1932, he recalled one distinguished-looking elderly gentleman. The guest was especially curious about the life cycles of the flowers and redwoods and kept Harry busy answering questions for over an hour. Returning to the park gate, the guest thanked his guide for his courteous treatment and said: "If you should happen to be in Santa Rosa someday, call and see me. My name is Burbank."[261]

Harry Staley passed away in 1941. Sadly, but perhaps fittingly, he died a few days after collapsing while taking a party on a tour of the Big Trees.[262]

A GREAT DISAPPOINTMENT

Opportunity for a presidential visit came again in 1901. This time, President William McKinley and his wife were on a western tour that was to bring them to Santa Cruz that May. Extravagant preparations were made for a banquet lunch at Big Trees Grove. When Mrs. McKinley fell ill, the president decided to stay at her bedside. The people of Santa Cruz had set their hearts on the president's visit, "and dismay was pictured on every face when it was learned at the eleventh hour that neither the President nor his wife could be present." Despite the disappointment, the townspeople carried out the program as it had been arranged. Serving in lieu of the president were members of his cabinet led by Secretary of State John Hay. The cabinet's party was driven to the grove by Milo Hopkins in an elegantly decorated landau festooned with a silk flag and ropes of red geraniums and white roses.[263] The dignitaries and their wives first stopped to have their photograph taken at the base of the General Grant Tree. A guide then hurriedly showed the cabinet through the grove, first walking them through the multi-trunk wonder Ingersoll's Cathedral and then on to the Fremont

On May 13, 1901, President William McKinley's cabinet members attended a luncheon at Big Trees Grove on his behalf. *Gilder Lehrman Institute.*

Tree, where fifteen or twenty members of the party entered the tree's hollow. The cabinet members then gathered in a shady glen for "a tempting luncheon, composed of Santa Cruz county wines, oranges from the south, ripe olives, sandwiches and various fruits gathered within a stone's throw of the spot. A bevy of pretty girls in spring gowns greeted the distinguished visitors and made them welcome." During the meal, the presidential train was transformed by the Native Daughters of the Golden West into a garden adorned with "smilax and garlands of roses over the exterior and piled bunches of roses, carnations, sweet peas, California poppies, and lilies in every corner."[264] The gift of a painting depicting the redwoods by local artist Frank Heath, titled *Nature's Temple*, was later shipped to the president as a memento of the visit that never was.[265]

Chapter 10

RIVALRY IN THE REDWOODS

We make our friends; we make our enemies;
but God makes our next door neighbor.
—C.K. Chesterton

In the early twentieth century, the Welch family began to face growing competition for the tourist dollar. In May 1902, Henry Cowell leased his land along the San Lorenzo River adjacent to Big Trees Grove for the establishment of a rival resort. Cowell had already begun logging his parcel. Leasing it allowed him to squeeze yet another source of income from the nearly cleared land. It is little surprise that Cowell was described as a "sordid materialist with a dollar-mark for a soul."[266] The following spring, the eighty-four-year-old Cowell was wounded in Merced by a gunshot inflicted on him by a disgruntled neighbor over a border dispute dating back many years. Cowell's death that August was attributed to the earlier wound, though some believed that the accidental death of his beloved daughter, Sarah, in a carriage accident just a few months before hastened his demise. Cowell, who owned tens of thousands of acres throughout California and beyond, left behind a fortune estimated at $3 million, equivalent today to nearly $90 million.[267]

The resort entrepreneur who leased a portion of the Big Trees from Cowell was Milo Hopkins. With a lease for a period of ten years at $250 per year, Hopkins quickly constructed a rustic clubhouse next to the railroad tracks.[268] The new resort became known variously as Cowell's Big

Trees, Cowell's Club House, Hopkins' Café and Hopkins' Big Trees. In order to compete with the Welch resort, Hopkins decided not to charge an admission fee. He and his wife, Alma, made money selling meals, redwood souvenirs, "bottles of pop, confectionery, [and] postcards."[269] He was also a noted cook and became famous for his barbecues. Hopkins became the Welch family's primary competitor through the 1920s. The intense rivalry between them, often contentious and sometimes humorous, became the stuff of local legend.

The jovial, rotund Milo Hopkins, a native of New York, came to California in about 1882. He arrived in Santa Cruz from Newcastle in Placer County in 1895. For many years, he operated the City Stables, a livery company in Santa Cruz. Working with Southern Pacific Railroad, he brought many visitors up Big Trees Road to the grove in his great "coach-and-six" known as Queen of the Pacific.[270] Years later, his daughter-in-law Mrs. George C. Hopkins recalled that often visitors "were so affected by the sight of the trees, they couldn't speak."[271]

The rivalry between Hopkins and the Welch brothers accelerated in July 1902 when the Southern Pacific chose to no longer stop its trains at Big Trees Grove. Instead, the railroad moved its stop a few hundred yards farther down the line to Hopkins's new establishment. The new Big Tree Station made evident that "the railroad company has no love for the Welch management of the Big Tree grove property."[272] During an event that August at Big Trees Grove in honor of the coronation of King Edward VII, the competition between the resorts was in full view.

> *This time a party had the advantage of being shown through the main grove by two of the Welch boys* [likely Stanly and Herman], *who know it "like a book," and one of them expressed the opinion that the railroad company had paid for and put in order what is now called the Cowell Grove and which is under the supervision of M.C. Hopkins. When the railroad train stopped in front of the Cowell Grove, and not the Welch Grove (in fact only one body of timber) we thought Mr. Welch was a real good guesser.*[273]

It didn't help matters that Hopkins's newspaper ads told visitors that they could enjoy viewing the Big Trees from his establishment, when in reality, the best of the grove belonged to his neighbors the Welch brothers.[274]

> [Tourists] *sat on the porch of the club-house and looked at Mr. Welch's trees. It should be stated that Mr. Welch had neglected to fence the side of*

Milo Hopkins and his grandson Stanley pose in front of the Club House on Cowell's Big Trees. *Courtesy of the Stewart family.*

The Club House at Cowell's Big Trees was built in 1902. Note the steep steps that led up to the train tracks. *Author's personal collection.*

DON'T MISS SEEING

THE BIG TREES

THIS FAMOUS GROVE of Giant Redwoods lies about six miles north of the City of Santa Cruz and is among the great curiosities of the Coast. These giants of the forest are reached by one of the most picturesque driveways in California. This highway penetrates to the very heart of the mountains, clinging to the hillsides, running along the lofty banks of the lovely San Lorenzo river and delighting the eye at every turn with some exquisite bit of mountain scenery.

Carriages, with careful drivers, for Big Trees and Santa Cruz reserved at Southern Pacific Ticket Office, 613 Market Street, San Francisco. Cal.

ADDRESS **M. C. HOPKINS,**

PROPRIETOR
CITY STABLES **SANTA CRUZ, CAL.**

Author's personal collection.

A staircase led down from Big Tree Station to the Club House at Cowell's Big Trees. *Courtesy of Frank Perry.*

Visitors pose by the Jumbo Tree. Note the visitors in the background viewing the Giant. *Courtesy of Frank Perry.*

A crowd of tourists await the train at Big Tree Station, circa 1910. *Courtesy of Ross Eric Gibson.*

his premises next to his neighbor. This he proceeded to do at once. A fence 12 feet high was erected and once more Mr. Welch was happy, for the tourists began to patronize him again. His triumph was shortlived. No sooner was the view cut off from the porch of the club-house than Mr. Hopkins began to think. His thoughts presently resulted in the arrival of carpenters. These men erected a handsome pavilion 25 feet high, with steps leading up to it and comfortable seats on its platform. Tourists can sit on the platform and have an unobstructed view of the wonders of nature as displayed in Mr. Welch's back yard. Meanwhile everybody in the vicinity of the big trees is waiting for Mr. Welch's next move and wondering what it will be.[275]

Perhaps in response to Hopkins's success, the Welch brothers tried different ways to entice visitors. An oft-told story is that the Fremont Tree was touted as a honeymoon suite to encourage more overnight stays. After all, the Fremont Tree was supposedly furnished as a room for a time, complete with wood floor, bed and wood stove. Mention of a blanket being draped across the entrance as late as 1879 implied that a caretaker may still have been using the tree's hollow as a residence.[276] Though no further evidence of its occupation or any advertisements of it being a hotel room has come to light, an article in the April 2, 1903 *Ogden [UT] Standard* describing a visit of the Mormon Tabernacle Choir gives some validity to the long-told story. A

Photographer William Sherer took this picture of his wife, Lulu, next to the Calling Card Tree at Cowell's Big Trees. *Santa Cruz Public Libraries, courtesy of Cynthia Mathews.*

lady in the group recounted being shown various trees in the grove, but one captured her attention. She was told that the Big Tree with the huge, burnt-out hollow at its base was called the "Bridal Chamber" House. The lady was not impressed and responded, "I should prefer something more romantic than an old tree, also more dainty."[277]

Meanwhile, Hopkins made further innovations. Starting in the summer of 1905, Hawaiian musicians entertained special groups.[278]

> *The music was furnished…by an orchestra composed of swarthy native Hawaiians, who played entirely on guitars and other stringed instruments, their national airs. Many of their selections were strange and weird, and to others they sang sweet-sounding songs in their native tongue, which no one understood, but which gave a pleasant effect to their music. This was a catchy innovation in the musical program.*[279]

Like the Welch brothers, Hopkins also tempted more organizations to host their large picnics at his resort by guaranteeing them a Big Tree dedication as a fitting finale of their event. One of Hopkins's attempts to anticipate visitor needs backfired. In preparation for a visit of six hundred Chinese tourists from San Francisco, Hopkins stocked up on tea, only to have a run on milk, coffee and soda pop so that "the Santa Cruz Creamery was kept busy bottling and delivering all day long to keep" up with the demand.[280] Hopkins's career as a resort proprietor was almost cut short. On April 18, 1906, he narrowly escaped death during the San Francisco earthquake. Awakened by a tremendous shaking in his fourth-floor room at San Francisco's St. Nicholas Hotel, Hopkins barely exited the building before the wall of an adjoining hotel fell through the ceiling.[281]

Chapter II

IN THE SHADOW OF THE BIG TREES

With crackling blows of axes sounding musically driven by strong arms,
Riven deep by the sharp tongues of the axes, there in the redwood forest dense,
I heard the mighty tree its death-chant chanting.

The choppers heard not, the camp shanties echoed not,
The quick-ear'd teamsters and chain and jack-screw men heard not,
As the wood-spirits came from their haunts of a thousand years to join the refrain,
But in my soul I plainly heard.
—Walt Whitman, "Song of the Redwood-Tree"

By the opening of the twentieth century, the logging of redwoods by Henry Cowell, within sight of the pristine Welch property, set up a stark contrast not lost on many visitors to Big Trees Grove. A visitor in 1902 recounted that

> *before reaching our destination we were to be tortured by the sight of thousands of acres from which every redwood of salable size had been cut, split and perverted into cash to add yet another million to the pockets of an already multi-millionaire [presumably Henry Cowell]. "Breathes there a man with soul so dead?" [W]e wondered at the sight of the charred stumps of fallen giants that were great trees when Rome was mistress of the world. This slaughter of aged Innocents still goes on in California. (Oh, the folly of it, in this arid State of all places!) where the land is owned*

by lumber dealers and not reserved by the Government or by men who find it more profitable to charge an admission fee to tourists like ourselves. But righteous anger against the rich old sinner who had devastated this region melted after we crossed the line of his vast possessions and entered his neighbor's territory, [Welch's Big Trees Grove] where redwoods in all their primeval grandeur still stood. [282]

The following year, another visitor expressed his fears for the future of the Big Trees:

This select forty acres will be sacredly preserved during the life time of a good old lady of eighty years [Anna Welch]. *But unless the government or state buys the land only the stumps of this wonderful forest will be here for the next generation to wonder at. Even while my guide showed me through this fenced part he called my attention to the sound of the woodman's maul "felling" similar trees not four hundred yards distant; felling them even for railroad ties.…To realize what this sublimest of Nature's works may look like after this old lady's death I had only to walk over a suspension foot bridge across the…[San Lorenzo] river…and [t]here on a single mutilated acre stand the charred stumps of 123 immense trees that were sacrificed a quarter of a century ago; evidence of our "great civilization."* [283]

Over the years, there were sporadic calls for the creation of parks to protect portions of the coast redwood and giant sequoia forests. A reporter once asked Henry Cowell his views on preservation: "Theoretically, Mr. Cowell believes it is a sin and a shame to wantonly destroy the trees which the Almighty has been so many years rearing for man. Speaking of the size of California trees he told of a tree he recently had felled which yielded 125 cords of wood." [284]

The first successful movement for government-sponsored protection was for the giant sequoias. The Yosemite Grant Act, signed by President Abraham Lincoln on June 30, 1864, reserved to the State of California not only Yosemite Valley but also the Mariposa Grove of giant sequoias. Protection of additional giant sequoia groves came in 1890 with the creation of Sequoia National Park, General Grant National Park and Yosemite National Park. The early protection for the giant sequoias is understandable since their lumber was not as prized as that of the redwood. Upon felling, giant sequoias often shattered. Their soft wood was good primarily for fence posts and shingles rather than construction lumber. The coast redwoods, on the other hand, were the ideal lumber. Imbued with tannic acid and lacking pitch, the redwood possesses a greater ability to withstand insects, disease and fire. As John Muir pointed out in 1897, "As timber, the redwood is too good to live."[285] As far back as 1876, one visitor pondered about the future of Big Trees Grove, stating that "somebody ought to buy that tract of land, and preserve it, and all that is on it, in its natural condition, as a public park."[286] Unfortunately, a government park to protect the coast redwoods remained elusive.

A SIGHT TO MAKE BACCHUS SHED TEARS

On the evening of October 7, 1899, crowds hurried to the western outskirts of San Jose to view the spectacle of fire racing across a ridge above Los Gatos. Among the spectators was photographer Andrew P. Hill.

I could see a great blaze at the base of the trees that seemed like a furnace. Then, one after the other, they were simply enveloped from the base to tip with flame, which leaped upwards with a velocity so great that it seemed unable to stop when it reached the top of the tree. Then, with one great bound, it continued, leaving tree and earth far behind, and exploding high in mid-air, lighting up the country for miles around.[287]

This fire, believed started accidentally by brush burning, proved especially destructive. Over two dozen residences were destroyed, including the home of writer Josephine Clifford McCrackin.[288] Also in the fire's path was Mare Vista Winery, owned by Emil E. Meyer. In the face of imminent danger, this winery owner proved resourceful.

It was like spontaneous combustion. The very air seemed on fire. But the men soon had a hose on the wine-vat near the south-west door, and, with a shout, manned the pump…and the hose was run out upon the roof. There were now one hose of water and two of claret. It was a sight to make Bacchus shed tears—this seeming waste of ruby-red glorious wine that was played upon the devouring flames.[289]

Approximately four thousand gallons of wine were pumped through the hoses. The young wine, hardly fermented, did the trick and stopped the progress of the conflagration.[290]

THE PHOTOGRAPH THAT LAUNCHED A MOVEMENT

Josephine Clifford McCrackin quickly realized this uniquely California story would prove irresistible. With her encouragement and that of her friend and fellow writer Bret Harte, a British publication known as *Wide World Magazine* chose to publish the thrilling episode. The dramatic scenes she described were documented by Pasadena-based naturalist Professor Charles Frederick Holder in his article "How a Forest Fire Was Extinguished with Wine" for the magazine's August 1900 edition. Photographer Andrew P. Hill, recommended by McCrackin, took views of the fire-devastated region. Part of Hill's plans also included taking photographs of living redwoods in order to demonstrate the immense size of the trees in the Santa Cruz Mountains.

Hill took a train ride to Big Trees Grove. As he began to set up his camera in front of the Giant, he was quickly confronted by a representative of the resort who ordered him to stop. The man declared that outsiders were not allowed to take photographs, as they were the province of the hotel.[291] Big Trees Grove also had a twenty-five-cent admission fee. Hill was incensed about having to make any payment to enter the grove. He indignantly explained that his photographs were being taken for a British publication and could only be a benefit to the grove owners since images of the Big Trees would be seen around the world. According to Hill, he was rudely dismissed from the grove, but not before he got a photograph for Holder's article. The identity of the man who confronted Hill remains in doubt. Some believe manager Joseph Ball was responsible, while others believe it was Stanly Welch. Judging from their personalities and later actions, Stanly seems the likelier candidate. Though we may never know for certain who the perpetrator was, the consequence of the confrontation was undeniable. Soon after the episode, Josephine Clifford McCrackin penned an editorial in the *Santa Cruz Sentinel* critical of the owners of Big Trees Grove, thereby launching a movement. Her March 7, 1900 piece titled "Save the Trees" was signed only with the appellation "An Old Californian":

> *I am not acquainted with Mr. Welch, but I think we all agree with Mr. Hill when he says that the course this gentleman takes is utterly un-American; and I add that it is un-Californian. And while I raise my feeble voice in protest against the selfishness that would debar others from looking at and enjoying one of God's greatest works merely because to this one man fell the piece of earth on which stand these trees, I beseech the people of this county*

This fuzzy photograph of the Giant was quickly taken by Andrew P. Hill for the August 1900 edition of the *Wide World Magazine*. *Courtesy of* Wide World Magazine.

and our neighbor-counties, indeed the people of all our State, to unite their voice with mine and make it loud enough, and strong enough, to reach our legislators and law-makers.[292]

Though McCrackin respected Welch's private property rights, judging by his disposition, she feared that he was capable of cutting the trees for firewood or fence rails if he could get enough money for them.

At this time, others called for giving federal government protection to the Calaveras Grove where the giant sequoias were first discovered. When a joint resolution to acquire Calaveras was introduced in the U.S. Congress, many Santa Cruzans asked, "Is it too late to include the Santa Cruz Big Trees in these negotiations?"[293] The fallout from the confrontation between Hill and the Welch family spawned fears that "if the Santa Cruz Big Trees do not become National property and reserved there is no telling what their destiny may be."[294] When Congress balked at the purchase price for the Calaveras Grove, the deal fell through. The slight chance that Big Trees Grove might also receive federal government protection also evaporated.

In the wake of McCrackin's editorial, locally the idea of preserving the redwoods gained momentum. Some concerned citizens wanted to acquire the Welch property for a proposed state park, but others had long been advocating for the preservation of another grove of Big Trees farther up the valley. Since the Welch family refused all overtures about their property, the focus of all preservation efforts quickly turned to the redwood forest outside Boulder Creek. Starting in May 1900, a group of women and men activists composed of academics, politicians and journalists began an extensive, statewide publicity campaign to save the redwoods. The newly formed Sempervirens Club turned its sights on acquiring the only other remaining grove of old-growth redwoods in the Santa Cruz Mountains. After a hard-fought two-year effort, the hopes of countless advocates were realized when the redwood park bill was signed into law in March 1901. In 1902, Big Basin opened as the state's first park.[295]

Chapter 12

A GIANT AMONG THE BIG TREES

*We should see to it that no man for speculative purposes or for mere temporary
use exploits the groves of great trees. Where the individuals and associations…
cannot preserve them, the state and if necessary the nation, should step in and
see to their preservation.*
—*address of President Theodore Roosevelt at Santa Cruz, California,
May 11, 1903*

In April 1903, President Theodore Roosevelt embarked upon a fourteen-thousand-mile rail tour of the American West. Begun as a political expedition, it became one of the most consequential presidential trips in American history.[296] Though the most lauded leg of the trip was Roosevelt's meeting with naturalist John Muir in Yosemite Valley, the president also visited many of the nation's most scenic landscapes. The lessons learned during his trip served him well. By the end of his presidency, Roosevelt had become known as the conservationist president, setting aside over 230 million acres of public land.

Santa Cruzans still keenly felt the disappointment of missing out on a visit from President McKinley two years before. When it was announced that President Roosevelt would make the city one of his stops, the citizens were determined to make it memorable. The highlight of the presidential visit would be a trip to the redwoods. After a two-hour trip from the Del Monte Hotel in Monterey, the president's train pulled into Santa Cruz on the morning of May 11. Roosevelt was welcomed by large and enthusiastic crowds as he was paraded through the downtown streets. In his brief address, given on Pacific Avenue, he congratulated the people for their efforts just the year before in creating the first redwood state park, Big Basin:

> *I am about to visit the grove of the great trees. I wish to congratulate you people of California…on what you have done to preserve these great trees. Cut down one of these giants and you cannot fill its place. The ages were their architects and we owe it to ourselves and to our children's children to preserve them.*[297]

In place of seeing the new state park, the presidential party boarded a train for the more easily accessible Big Trees Grove. Arriving at Cowell's Big Trees, the Secret Service reconnoitered the area and the Naval Reserves stood guard while the party filed past. An alfresco breakfast for eighty guests awaited them near the Fremont Tree at the Welch resort. At the table, "a huge bouquet of lady slippers, gathered this morning on the river bank was placed immediately in front of the President, but afterwards removed to permit all present to have an uninterrupted view."[298] Twenty young ladies from Santa Cruz High School helped serve a meal of broiled steaks, Spanish beans, salad, biscuits, strawberries, coffee, cake and Ben Lomond wine. Roosevelt claimed the steak was the best he had eaten since his cowboy days. Fred Swanton pointed out to the president that the woman who prepared the Spanish beans was Mrs. José Maria Guiereres,[299] a mother of thirty-four children. Amused, the president remarked, "She ought to be made a President of some association. I don't know what."

As the band played lively airs, Mayor David Curtis Clark told the president that the young ladies hoped to hear him give a little speech. No speech had been planned, but the president, who was "bubbling over with good humor," happily agreed.[300] He glanced to his right at the group of Big Trees called the Three Sisters, calling attention to the one with a fire-scarred hollow base covered in a blizzard of calling cards and notes. Though the president complimented the people of Santa Cruz for preserving the redwoods, he also admonished them for the unfortunate local tradition of placing signs and calling cards on the trees.[301]

> *This is the first glimpse I have ever had of the big trees, and I wish to pay the highest tribute I can to the state of California, to those private citizens, and associations of citizens who have cooperated with the state in preserving these wonderful trees for the whole nation.…All of us ought to*

On May 11, 1903, President Theodore Roosevelt posed before the Giant. *Courtesy of the California History Room, California State Library, Sacramento, California.*

want to see nature preserved....Above all the rash creature who wishes to leave his name to mar the beauties of nature should be sternly discouraged. Take those cards pinned up on that tree; they give an air of the ridiculous to this solemn and majestic grove. (Applause) To pin those cards up there is as much out of place as if you tacked so many tin cans up there. I mean that literally. You should save the people whose names are there from the reprobation of every individual by taking down the cards at the earliest possible moment; and do keep these trees, keep all the wonderful scenery of this wonderful state unmarred by the vandalism or the folly of man....Put a stop to any destruction of or any marring of the wonderful and beautiful

The outdoor bar at the Three Sisters, circa 1890s. *Special Collections, University Library, University of California–Santa Cruz (Santa Cruz Historical Photographs Collection).*

gifts that you have received from nature, that you ought to hand on as a precious heritage to your children and your children's children....I do hope that it will be your object to preserve them as nature made them and left them for the future.[302]

The crowd responded with shouts of "Amen! Amen!" When the meal concluded, Roosevelt indicated to the mayor that he wished to walk through the grove without a crowd but added, "That I love you not less, but the trees more."[303] The president then walked over to the Giant to pose for a photograph. He next set out arm in arm with his companion, Professor Nicholas Murray Butler, president of Columbia University, for a fifteen-minute walk through the grove. There is a story that spectators saw the president lie down briefly midway through the walk—whether to take a better look at the towering Big Trees or take a quick nap, no one knows for sure.

In the president's absence, the organizers of the event quickly began to tear cards and notes down from the surrounding trees "without even consulting the wishes of the lordly proprietor of the grove, Mr. Welch."[304]

The dignitaries then gathered at the base of a particularly beautiful Big Tree with a straight trunk a few hundred feet west of the hotel. The president and Professor Butler met the rest of the party at the flag-draped tree. Roosevelt was asked if he objected to having a tree named in his honor. The president replied, "Not at all, but on the contrary, would consider it a great honor." When newspaper photographers requested the president pose for a photograph before his namesake tree, he insisted that all the dignitaries present stand by his side for the picture taking.[305] Then the mayor pulled aside the flag, revealing the name "Roosevelt" embossed on a large metal sign nailed to the bark.[306] The president thanked the assembled crowd and said he was deeply touched and flattered. Upon seeing the sign, measuring at least two feet long and five or six inches wide, the president asked if he could make one suggestion. He walked up to the tree and, holding his fingers in the shape of a small rectangle, asked if the sign could be removed and substituted for a smaller one. He hoped not to offend his hosts but stipulated that a sign bearing his name "should not be more than three-quarters of an inch by an inch and a half in diameter" because he did not want to mar the beauty and symmetry of the tree.[307]

A different, livelier account of the tree dedication comes from one of the photographers present, Robert Lee Dunn. After the sign was revealed, Dunn claimed Roosevelt shouted, "Take it down! That's nothing but desecration. Tear it down, I say! Tear it down and put up my card instead." The photographer claimed someone took the president's calling card and affixed it to the tree in place of the large "Roosevelt" sign.[308] The truth is probably somewhere in between. Despite the president's stern admonition during his visit about hanging large signs and hundreds of calling cards on the Big Trees, this practice persisted at the grove for several decades.

On his way back to the banquet table, the president walked up to the Fremont Tree, which he thoroughly inspected, inside and out. While the party was occupied in the grove, the Native Daughters of the Golden West added to the decoration already on the presidential train. In addition to both sides of the train being adorned with white flowers arranged in the letter R, so much more patriotic bunting, redwood branches, woodwardia, carnations and roses covered the cab that the engineer was further hidden from view.[309]

The year following his visit, Roosevelt advocated for the naming of a tree at the grove. The president wrote a letter endorsing the plan to name

Despite the president's wishes, the large "Roosevelt" sign remained on the tree dedicated in his honor for many years. *Courtesy of Ross Eric Gibson.*

a tree in the memory of Nebraskan J. Sterling Morton, former secretary of agriculture and, in 1872, founder of Arbor Day. Roosevelt said Morton deserved the honor for "the way he promoted tree-planting and forestry."[310] Unfortunately, we do not know which tree in the grove was bestowed this honor.

Chapter 13

BLUEJACKETS AND JACK TARS

Don't let the sailor boys go away thinking us unhospitable or ungenerous.
—Santa Cruz Morning Sentinel, *May 2, 1908*

It might seem strange at first to find sailors in a redwood forest, but at Big Trees Grove, it became a tradition from early on. Local legend claims that sailors who jumped ship in Santa Cruz made their way to the San Lorenzo Valley to take safe shelter with old pioneer Isaac Graham. On his rancho, they supposedly hid within the burnt-out hollow of what later became known as the Fremont Tree. As a port city, Santa Cruz occasionally hosted visits from U.S. naval vessels. The earliest documented naval visit to Big Trees Grove was in 1896 when Admiral Lester Beardslee and sailors from the USS *Philadelphia* enjoyed a mountain outing.[311]

But by far the most famous contingent of sailors visiting Big Trees Grove took place in 1908 when the Great White Fleet visited Santa Cruz. The term "Great White Fleet" was a nickname for the U.S. Atlantic fleet that made the first around-the-world cruise by a contingent of steam-powered steel battleships. The forty-three-thousand-mile, fourteen-month circumnavigation was the idea of President Theodore Roosevelt to display American naval dominance of the seas and remains one of the greatest achievements of the peacetime navy.[312]

Santa Cruz was one of the twenty ports of call for the fleet. On May 3, 1,500 bluejackets boarded trains for the trip up San Lorenzo Canyon.

Six long trains carried the men to the grove....On the creek the trout fisherman of Santa Cruz county had out their lines....Along the track were masses of wild flowers and the bushy birch showed wide bonnets of blue to the men from the sea. All this was good to vary the monotony of the cruise and the sailors drank in the mountain air and the soft lines of the hills and mountains with lungs and eyes that had been hungry for such refreshment.

After half an hour on the train the sailors and marines were disembarked at the foot of several perpendicular giants. At the bottom of the railroad embankment the lunch was spread. But the trees attracted the lads ahead of the food. The nobles of the forest giants were inclosed behind a high fence. Of course, the builder of the fence did not try to erect his palisade to[o] high as to shut off the view of the tops of the timber....The sailors were admitted without price....[Then] the wardens of the woods took the boys among the tiers of trees and explained the various virtues and merits of each specimen, how many hands high it might be and whether it had a sunny or a sullen disposition, as a groom might do at the horse show. "They're tallest things I've ever seen," cried a truthful tar from Rhode Island, "and they are growing every day, too. They'll be taller yet when our grandchildren come out in a hundred years to look at them," added another, soberly....

From the [G]iant the path of the guides lead to the General Fremont.... [Next in] the line of march lay General Sherman, the Roosevelt and a

In 1908, sailors of the Great White Fleet visited the grove. *Arthur C. Pillsbury Foundation, www. acpillsburyfoundation.org. Special Collections, University Library, University of California–Santa Cruz (Santa Cruz Historical Photographs Collection).*

number of other dignities. Some humorous but irreverent jackies from the Rhode Island selected a small birch tree and dedicated it with unction to some unpopular officer of that vessel. As General Fremont had had his photo taken before the huge redwood so did the sailors....In the park there is a curio merchant who sells various articles made from redwood bark and wood and picture postcards showing the trees. He found a ready market for his trophies of the forest among the sailors. The table where the cards may be addressed and mailed was always crowded with groups of filial bluejackets letting home and mother know of their adventures in the golden west.[313]

The luncheon consisted of sixteen quarters of beef and twenty barbecued sheep along with "coffee, potato salad, beans by the 100 gallons, together with olives and relishes, were served on the tables and the feasters were plentifully supplied with claret and sauterne."[314] It was said that all the pretty girls of Santa Cruz were at the picnic.[315] A platform for the band of the USS *Vermont* was erected on the stump of a felled giant surrounded by nine sapling

In 1908, a sailor from the USS *Montana* posed at the entrance of the Fremont Tree. *Courtesy of Traci Bliss.*

redwoods, called the Nine Muses. After the luncheon, "the younger of the ladies who had served the jackies became escorts for them in second tours of the grove. By the time the boy[s] left the park they had twists in their necks from constantly trying to espy the tops of the monsters of the forest."[316] Before leaving, a group of seventy-six sailors crowded into the hollow of the Fremont Tree.[317] As a memento, each sailor was given a souvenir napkin ring and a bouquet of flowers.

At the conclusion of the sailors' tour, one of the monarchs of the forest was named for the commander of the fleet, "Fighting Bob" Evans.[318] One bluejacket noticed that the grove did not contain a Big Tree named for Secretary of War and presidential candidate William Howard Taft. The guide told him "they were waiting for one to grow big enough around."[319] In July 1909, the Santa Cruz Chamber of Commerce sent an invitation to President Taft to come visit Big Trees Grove to have a tree named in his honor.[320] That visit did not materialize, and it remains uncertain if a tree was ever dedicated to him.[321]

The navy came again to Big Trees Grove in 1919 when 300 officers and 2,220 seamen made the trip up San Lorenzo Canyon.[322]

Visitors got a "Big Trees" postmark for their postcards at an outdoor post office near the Fremont Tree. *Author's personal collection.*

[Admiral Hugh Rodman's] *car halted before the towering heavy-branched reaches of the Cathedral. Then, in the calm stillness, broken only by the hum of the automobile and the quiet murmur of the forest, William T. Jeter, chairman of the committee, raised from the massive trunk of the Cathedral an American flag, disclosing a paneled inscription to the effect that one of the great monarchs of California's outdoors was dedicated in honor of the Admiral, his ships, officers and men.*[323]

An engraved tablet was placed on the tree. The tablet, made of brass from one of the obsolete naval guns, was dedicated to the officers and men of the U.S. Pacific Fleet who passed through the Panama Canal in the summer of 1919. Before departing, two of the presiding captains were presented with redwood burl nut bowels and nut crackers for use in the officers' mess rooms.[324] The tree honored during this visit later became known simply as the U.S. Navy Tree.

Chapter 14

THE IRON MASTER ADMIRES THE BIG TREES

Many thousands of people, including princes and presidents and eminent men from all over the world, have visited the Santa Cruz big trees, and the testimony of all has been that no one who has the opportunity should fail to see those stupendous and awe-inspiring specimens of nature's handiwork.
—David Starr Jordan, president of Stanford University, San Francisco Call, *May 28, 1909*

O ne of the most eminent men of the day came to Big Trees Grove on March 11, 1910. Steel magnate and philanthropist Andrew Carnegie came to Santa Cruz to see the new library on Church Street. After inspecting the $20,000 building that he gifted to the town, Carnegie, his wife and daughter headed by automobile up San Lorenzo Canyon to the grove. The party, invited by library board president Frank Bliss, initially stopped at Cowell's Big Trees.[325] One of the first trees the distinguished party encountered was covered with dozens of personal calling cards. Carnegie was informed that when President Roosevelt visited the grove in 1903, he voiced his displeasure of the local practice and asked that the cards be taken down. Carnegie paused a moment before the tree and then took out a card, saying "that he and Roosevelt were the best of friends, but that they had experienced two or three disputes before, and he presumed that they could stand another, and with these words he fastened his card upon the tree." The party then walked to the Welch family resort.[326] Carnegie was shown the famous

In 1910, millionaire steel magnate Andrew Carnegie, the white bearded gentleman seated at the back table, was an honored guest. *Santa Cruz Public Libraries.*

Fremont Tree, whereupon he exclaimed that he "was too young to vote for Fremont but, thank God, I voted for Lincoln."[327]

Local journalist Josephine Clifford McCrackin described the benefactor as a slender-built elderly gentleman with a genial face and beaming smile.[328] Carnegie stopped at the General Grant Tree to have his photograph taken. Figuring that he looked small in comparison to the Big Tree, he piled up leaves into a little mound on which he posed for the camera. As the party continued their walk, Carnegie asked and received from the guide some redwood seeds to take back to his estate in Scotland, Skibo Castle. Carnegie was especially pleased to see the tree named in honor of former president Roosevelt. Upon approaching the tree, he removed his hat and reportedly said, "Hello, Theodore, how are you?" He then declared that it was "as fine a tree as he is a man....He is a straight and upright man and towers as this tree does. He is the foremost man of our time....There is no sham about Theodore Roosevelt."[329]

On his outdoor dancing pavilion, Milo Hopkins spread a picnic-style steak luncheon for the fifty honored guests. Upon seeing the flag of Scotland waving above his seat and Scotch heather adorning his place setting, Carnegie was taken aback and said, "I am perfectly overcome. I will remember these Big Trees always, but more still will I remember the big hearts of your people." Carnegie further stated, "Several times have I murmured to myself today, 'The groves were God's first temples,' and I do not believe any temple ever reared by the hand of man can be considered in the same place with this before us." The chamber of commerce then presented him with a small baking soda can containing a two-year-old redwood seedling. Carnegie declared that he would plant it at his estate in Scotland. Rising to his feet, Carnegie held the can in his hand and said, "This tree will certainly grow. Everything grows that I get a hold of." He was asked what name he would give to the tree. He responded, "It shall be called 'The First Citizen in the United States." Then he noticed that the can contained two seedlings and added, "You don't mind my making a dividend of 100 per cent at this time, do you….But really I can't help it. Everything doubles in my hands." He continued, noting that "my little daughter is my head gardener, and she will put them both in her garden. I am sure that they will both grow in good old Scotland."[330]

The program concluded with a performance of Scottish songs. Then, at the request of Mrs. Carnegie, all present rose to their feet, crossed arms to join hands and sang in unison "Auld Land Syne." A group photograph was taken with Carnegie in the center holding the American and Scottish flags crossed in his arms.[331] Later in her journal, twelve-year-old Margaret recorded her impression of Big Trees Grove: "We were shown all the biggest trees…and our inclination was to talk in whispers. I felt as if I were in church."[332]

Chapter 15

THE SQUARED CIRCLE

Good fences make good neighbors.
—Robert Frost, "The Mending Wall," 1914

As the competition between Hopkins and the Welch brothers grew, so, too, did the fence, eventually reaching fourteen feet high. One commentator noted that "the holes, deep ones, are dug, and they run dangerously near to the Welch outbuildings, so near as to cut in two parts the Welch gate receipts."[333] Hopkins was better situated to take advantage of both railroad traffic and the new automobile tourism. Across from the Club House, he added a set of rustic cabins. By 1910, Hopkins was renting bungalows at rates of $2.50 per night or $15.00 by the week.[334] Day trips to the grove were also made easier with the operation of auto stages that ran daily from the beach. Gustav Rohrer operated a bus line that ran from the Casa del Rey Hotel to the Big Trees from 1914 to 1918.[335] A 1916 advertisement touted twice-daily $0.75 comfortable auto sightseeing round trips.[336] One visitor described his trip up Big Trees Road as

a run through canyons on precipices skirting mountain sides, almost raising my hair and turning the few black ones that I still have gray when making a short turn around some point or cliff on this, very narrow road, barely escaping a collision with a machine coming from the opposite direction on this crooked road where at times I could look down the mountain side for nearly a thousand feet and see a trout stream winding its course among the huge rocks that [had] fallen from its side, or looking upward hundreds of feet see more rocks and trees that looked rather threatening to a tender foot....

There are no guard rails on these very dangerous roads as we merrily roll along with a margin of only a few feet between us and eternity....Before entering these mountains we were warned to blow or sound our horn at every turn and not run faster than 10 miles an hour....Leaving the big trees we again took to the mountain roads, passing several traffic police who were having a good business catching violators of traffic and road regulations on the mountain highway.[337]

Both Big Tree resorts faced a new competitor for tourists after the establishment of the state's first redwood park, Big Basin, in 1902. From its inception, Big Basin was far larger than Big Trees Grove. The new park located outside Boulder Creek initially encompassed 3,601 acres, and by 1908, another 3,980 acres had been added to it. Despite its larger size, Big Basin attracted just over two thousand visitors each year during this period. The additional fifteen-mile journey up winding mountain roads and a lack of facilities probably contributed to its slower growth.[338] For at least a little while longer, the larger crowds and more intense competition for redwood tourists continued to be between the Welch brothers and Milo Hopkins in Felton.

Another coup for the Welch brothers came in 1910 with the visit of boxer James J. Jeffries, heavyweight champion from 1899 until 1905. Jeffries was planning a comeback. In April 1910, he set up a training camp at Ben Lomond's Hotel Rowardennan for his coming fight with Jack Johnson, the first black heavyweight champion. Jeffries was called the "Great White Hope" in anticipation of being the white man to win back the title.[339] In hopes of further solidifying his fame, Jeffries and his entourage planned a visit to Big Trees Grove,

where the ceremony of dedicating one [a tree] in his honor will be carried out with fully as much pomp and splendor as the exercises which marked like events when General Fremont, General Grant, Theodore Roosevelt and

Opposite, top: The American Library Association luncheon at Cowell's Big Trees in 1911. *Courtesy of the University of Illinois at Urbana-Champaign, University of Illinois, Archives, American Library Association Archives.*

Opposite, middle: By 1910, five stages ran daily from the Casino at the beach to the Toll House at the entrance to Cowell's Big Trees. *Courtesy of the San Lorenzo Valley Museum.*

Opposite, bottom: An automobile fording the San Lorenzo River near the swinging bridge, circa 1920. *Courtesy of the Santa Cruz Museum of Art and History.*

Grover Cleveland had giants of the forest christened in their honor....Jeff will have the distinction of being the first man of the gloves to be honored thusly. Poets, presidents and statemen were led into the great old grove in the past and had homage paid them by the multitude, but never before did this lot fall to a fighter. Even when the Queensberry game is dead and gone the name of Jeffries will be revered. It will be carved in one of nature's halls of fame and the members of future generations who never heard the name of Jeffries mentioned will learn about him if it is their good fortune to visit the historic big trees.[340]

One local commentator brought up a pertinent question that April: "Suppose on the Fourth of July the black should win? Will that lordly sentinel then be renamed the Jack Johnson?"[341] At the so-called Fight of the Century in Reno, Jeffries was knocked out by Johnson in the fifteenth round.[342] It is not known if the tree continued to bear the name Jeffries.

For years, Hopkins railed against the locks that Stanly Welch placed on the gate to Big Trees Grove. In August 1911, Hopkins "did the George Washington act at the Big Trees." However, he did not cut down a cherry tree or a redwood.

He simply battered down the gate which leads from the Cowell Grove into the Welch grove. A large Yellowstone touring party had been at his grove and passed through to see the trees in the Welch grove when Welch locked the gate on the party so they could not get back to Hopkins's reserve and return to their train. "Hop" was angry for it is said the same trick was turned once before this season. So he armed himself with an ax, and when he got through there was a clear passage way for the tourists for "Hop" proved to be proficient with the ax. It is alleged that [Stanly] Welch was behind the fence and struck Hopkins upon the arm spraining it quite badly, after which he disappeared.[343]

Hopkins minimized the incident, saying that it amounted to nothing. But this would not be the last such incident. In October 1918, Hopkins escorted a honeymoon couple, Dr. F.H. and Mrs. Phillips from Nevada, into the Welch portion of Big Trees Grove. When Hopkins was about to photograph the honeymooners, they were confronted by Stanly Welch, who ordered them to stop and leave his grove.

Hopkins refused on the ground that he had offered the admission price, only to have it refused. Then, according to Hopkins, his old-time adversary threw a piece of wood at him. Hopkins ducked this and Dr. Phillips took a hand in the controversy, landing a punch strong enough on Welch's jaw to lay him out. Welch arose and walking over to a basket near-by took out a revolver and pointing it at the trio ordered them off the grounds.[344]

No one was injured, but Hopkins did swear a complaint charging Stanly Welch with battery for striking him with a heavy walking can. The judge subsequently released Welch on his own recognizance.[345] Some locals thought that the competition would be good for the grove and might possibly lead to it being purchased by the railroad or becoming a public park someday. Instead, it led to more divisiveness.[346] "For reasons unknown to the owners of the forest, they have incurred the enmity of the people of Santa Cruz, who, the Welches claim, have sought in one way and another to drive them from their location and close up their establishment."[347]

Preservation of the grove was a constant source of expense for the Welch family. In addition to the taxes, the Welches hired guards and guides.[348] Through the 1920s, the Welches went back and forth on whether to sell Big

In 1916, two friends from Sacramento made Cowell's Big Trees a stop on their 760-mile bicycle ride across Northern California. *The Center for Sacramento History.*

Female motorists visit the Club House at Cowell's Big Trees, circa 1915. *Courtesy of the Santa Cruz Museum of Art and History.*

Trees Grove for its lumber or sell it to parties interested in its development or preservation. One of the heirs told the local newspaper in 1902 that it was probable that a one-hundred-room hotel would be built near the grove by eastern capitalists.[349] Such a hotel never materialized. At one point, Herman Welch reportedly met with lumber interests in San Francisco to dicker over a price for the timber. Joseph Welch Jr. said that if they lost income, they would "be compelled to do something that will make land remunerative, or, if need be, cut down the trees, in which we all have a pride. It will not be pleasant for us to do so, but if we are deprived of receiving any return from our investment, what are we going to do?"[350]

Chapter 16

HOLLYWOOD COMES TO THE BIG TREES

Santa Cruz is coming into its own as a moving picture center.
—Santa Cruz Evening News, *March 9, 1917*

The beauty of Big Trees Grove attracted a new industry in the early twentieth century. From 1911 to 1924, the grove was used as backdrop for over a dozen silent movies, thus spreading the grove's fame in a new way. The first of these movies was *A Diamond in the Rough* in 1911, a typical love melodrama of the era that's most interesting aspect to locals was the appearance of Henry Cowell's favorite ox team. In 1915, western star William S. Hart came to Big Trees Grove to direct and star in the movie *The Primal Lure.* Hart was one of the most popular and highest-earning leading men of the era. Using redwoods to build a stockade, the New York Motion Picture Company erected a replica of a frontier Canadian trading post on Cowell's property.[351] Santa Cruz's spectacular mountain scenery and mild climate began to entice more filmmakers. In 1916, Mayor Fred Howe traveled to Los Angeles to lobby movie companies to film in Santa Cruz. A direct result of his trip was the decision by the Jesse L. Lasky Company to choose the Santa Cruz redwoods as the setting for its next film, the oddly titled *Trail of the Lonesome Pine.* Lauded director Cecil B. DeMille and his twenty-seven-man crew filmed at various locations on Cowell's land.[352] At the conclusion of this feature, the director was recognized by the Santa Cruz Chamber of Commerce by having one of the mammoth redwoods named in his honor.[353] DeMille returned to Big Trees Grove in 1917 to film perhaps the best known of the movies that used the grove as a setting, *A Romance of the Redwoods*. The movie starred the most famous actress of the era, Mary Pickford. At the conclusion of her picture, Pickford was also honored in the Santa Cruz tradition.

> *It is the custom in the big tree forest near Santa Cruz, where Mary Pickford's picture*, A Romance of the Redwoods *was staged to name each one of the giants after some prominent person who has visited there. Theodore Roosevelt, General Grant, Ex-President Taft and a number of other celebrities have trees named after them in these wilds, each name being engraved on a brass plate and tacked to the base of the tree....She was asked to select one of the enormous trees, but Miss Pickford refused to accept any of them. Instead, she chose a young redwood, only a foot in circumference, which seemed a mere dwarf among the giants, and requested that this little tree be named after her.*[354]

Unfortunately, the locations of both the DeMille and Pickford trees remain unknown.

During the filming of Hart's movie *"Blue Blazes" Rawden*, the star displayed his physical prowess by reportedly cutting down a redwood giant about 250 feet high and several feet in diameter. The movie begins with Hart cutting a tree, but the location of the tree or its species is uncertain.[355] During the filming of Hart's third movie at Big Trees Grove, *The Testing Block*, the star provided a special entertainment for the locals. Several cowboys of the company staged a miniature rodeo in the public square in front of the Felton hotel.[356]

More thrilling than the rodeo feats or any of the scenes filmed for the movies was the real-life adventure of stunt pilot Richard Grace during the 1923 filming of the Tom Mix movie *Eyes of the Forest*. The story is about a forest ranger trying to prove a woman innocent of murder by using his airplane to track down the true villain. As Grace flew over the grove for the last few aerial views, he dove down as close to the treetops as possible, while expert cameraman Norman Devoe took the shots. Twice they swooped between rock ledges and were making their final sweep of the treetops when

> *without the slightest warning, my motor quit—absolutely dead. I was headed directly toward one of the bluffs. Below was a little clearing, surrounded by trees. To hit one of those huge redwoods—or the bluff— or to side-slip into the clearing—those three alternatives were offered. I*

pulled the switch and, turning to Devoe, yelled "We're going to crash; sit down!" At two hundred feet from the ground I looked around again. He was standing and still grinding the camera. "Sit down—quick!" I warned. He smiled and nodded, but continued to "shoot" the crash. With a terrific impact we hit, and for a few seconds there were struts, wings, wires and dirt flying in all directions....I escaped injury with the exception of a broken vein in the head. Devoe had a few patches of skin missing. Peculiarly, although the camera had broken from its mount, it was undamaged and we got, I dare say, the first shot of an airplane in an actual crash ever recorded.[357]

Perhaps the most unique film of the era associated with the grove is 1924's *The Last Man on Earth*. The film takes place in the future setting of 1950 when a disease called Masculitis wiped out all virile men. Despite the advantages of a world ruled by women and without war, society must locate at least one man to ensure the continuation of humankind. A posse that has searched the world over for ten years finally locates a man unaffected

Lobby card from the Tom Mix movie *Eyes of the Forest*, during which stunt pilot Dick Grace was forced into a harrowing crash landing. *Wikimedia Commons.*

by the plague. They find the hermit deep in the forest and living in the hollow of an immense tree because his sweetheart jilted him for another man years before. The tree used in the movie is none other than the famed redwood the Fremont Tree. The man is dragged back to civilization against his will. He is sold to the U.S. government for $10 million, and then his fate is to be decided by a boxing match held on the floor of the U.S. Senate. During the match, he suddenly spots his former sweetheart. They rush into each other's arms, and all the past is forgiven. They marry, and the subsequent births of their twin sons saves the world.[358]

Chapter 17

A NEW CHAPTER BEGINS

When one tugs at a single thing in nature,
he finds it attached to the rest of the world.
——John Muir

The year 1928 began a new chapter for Big Trees Grove. The State of California formed a commission to collect data on potential park sites. A consultant to the commission was landscape architect Frederick Law Olmsted Jr. As a student of architecture in 1886, Olmsted visited the grove with his famous father. That trek was young Olmsted's first glimpse of the redwoods, and he remembered it fondly.[359] He agreed with his fellow commission member Daniel Hull that

> *the Welch grove is certainly worthy of consideration as a scenic and recreational spot. Within three hours by automobile from San Francisco, and one-half that time from the inland towns like San Jose, it serves a real recreational need and is certainly of state park caliber. It is to be hoped that this area may always be available for the enjoyment of the public.*[360]

Though state park status for the grove did not materialize, the idea of finally making the grove a public park inspired others.[361]

One of the most dedicated advocates of preserving the grove was William Jeter. The former Santa Cruz mayor, former lieutenant governor of California and thirty-five-year president of Santa Cruz County Bank played a pivotal role. In a July 18, 1928 article in the *Santa Cruz Evening Sentinel*, Jeter claimed that Joseph Warren Welch always intended that the

> *trees, plant life, shrubbery and undergrowth should be perpetuated and maintained in their natural state until the tract could be disposed of for public enjoyment under restrictions to effectively assure such maintenance. His wish in this regard was faithfully respected after his death in the '70's, by his widow up to the time of her death in 1905, and subsequently by the Welch heirs down to the present time.*

By 1928, the Welch family was anxious to quit the resort business and soon entered negotiations with Santa Cruz County for purchase of the forty-acre parcel of Big Trees. Back in 1902, Stanly Welch deeded his interest in the property to his brother Herman. After Herman's death in 1926, Joseph Jr. took over his brother's portion of the estate. With the controlling interest, Joseph Jr. represented the family's interests.[362] Though many prominent citizens advocated for the purchase, it almost fell through when the county was unable to meet the Welches' initial $200,000 asking price. Though the price was negotiated down to $75,000, the success of a deal remained uncertain. Coming to the rescue was the Jeter family. As William Jeter was losing his battle with cancer, his wife, Jennie, helped call in her husband's remaining political favors to obtain the needed funds.[363] Thanks to Jeter's connections, the cooperation of Joseph Welch Jr. and the support of the community, finally, in 1930, Big Trees Grove officially became Santa Cruz County Big Trees Park. The old Welch resort buildings remained standing but unused.

In 1928, change also came to the other side of the grove. Milo Hopkins turned over management of the Club House at Cowell's Big Trees to his son George. Though George was ably assisted by his son Stanley, the tourist business declined during the Great Depression.[364] In the spring of 1940, heavy rains brought on a mud slide that blocked the Southern Pacific rail line through the mountains. The high estimated cost of recovery led the railroad to abandon the line from Oakland, cutting off a still important artery of the grove's tourist trade.[365] When Southern Pacific claimed out-of-state passengers would happily take the extra step to transfer by bus from a branch line to reach Big Trees Grove, an article in the *Riptide* that spring countered by saying that

> *when the railroad no longer goes to the Big Trees, the Big Trees DIE as a Santa Cruz tourist attraction….With abandonment of the Southern Pacific's*

William T. Jeter stands at the base of a Big Tree. *Special Collections, University Library, University of California–Santa Cruz (Santa Cruz Historical Photographs Collection).*

mountain railroad line, this community from a national standpoint—loses its greatest asset. With all deference to our beaches, mountains, climate and many other features, we lose our only claim to nationwide recognition when we take our Big Trees off the tourist pathway—the railroad....With rail connection gone, the Big Trees is just another picnic grove for the home folks and the week-ending California motorist![366]

The final blow came with the advent of World War II. In 1941, George's son Stanley joined the army, and with the Third Battalion, he fought in North Africa and Italy, taking part in the Allied landing at Anzio and the battle at Cassino. In his last letter home, Stanley confidently told his parents, "We have the Krauts pretty much on the run." In August 1944, Stanley was killed in fighting just outside Rome.[367]

Tastes changed after the war. With the opening of Highway 17 over the Santa Cruz Mountains in 1940, the newer auto tourist camps had begun to draw more visitors. The Cowell family retained ownership of the property containing Hopkins's resort and employed a caretaker to oversee the abandoned structures. Next door, the old Welch resort buildings suffered a similar fate. The county let the forlorn hotel buildings stand idle, and they, too, soon began to deteriorate.[368]

Not only were the last vestiges of the hotel era at the grove disappearing but so, too, was one of the founding families. During his lifetime, Henry Cowell so worried about fortune hunters that he threatened disinheritance if his children married. Five of Cowell's children lived to adulthood. Ernest was the only to marry but remained childless. By 1950, the last living descendant of Henry Cowell was his son Samuel H. "Harry" Cowell. Samuel was an avid outdoorsman and expert horseman. His love of nature reached its pinnacle when at the age of ninety-two he decided to donate 1,623 acres of land for a new park. The land bordering the San Lorenzo River included the site of the abandoned Cowell's Big Trees resort. Logged by his father over fifty years prior, the property was now covered with young, second-growth redwoods. Samuel Cowell's generous act, however, came with a couple of contingencies. He wanted his donated land combined with the neighboring county park and the entire parcel made into a California state park. The final requirement was the naming of the new park. Samuel insisted that it

Ruins of the hotel at Big Trees Grove, circa 1930s. *Courtesy of the California History Room, California State Library, Sacramento, California.*

bear the name of his father. In 1954, Henry Cowell Redwoods State Park opened to the public. The name of the new park set up the curious irony of a redwood park being named in honor of a man who probably cut down more redwoods in the San Lorenzo Valley than anyone else.

Over the past sixty years, Henry Cowell Redwoods State Park has become a popular destination, growing to 4,650 acres with over 1.1 million visitors annually. Today, the park consists of the 40 acres of the former Welch's Big Trees Grove as well as vibrant, second-growth redwoods on the former Cowell's Big Trees and Fall Creek's IXL lime works. The park also contains riparian habitat along the San Lorenzo River and a portion of the sandhills ecosystem, a raised ancient seabed home to many rare species found nowhere else in the world. Evolving scientific understanding provides the park's new visitors with a fuller appreciation of the area's habitats and species and their importance in our changing world.

None of this would have been possible without the foresight of Joseph Warren Welch. His decision in 1867 to save a grove of towering coast redwoods as a public picnic ground set the stage for preservation. The grove's existence is proof that the act of a single person can have a profound impact on all of us. Though Big Trees Grove suffered some of the ill effects of commercialization, the old-growth portion of the grove survived its resort era pretty well intact. The tens of thousands of visitors drawn to Big Trees Grove helped spread word not only about the redwoods' beauty and amazing attributes but also the threats they faced. Later, the selfless acts of others combined to give us the park we enjoy today. The grove continues to attract people from across the nation and around the world. Today's visitors, like their predecessors, have the opportunity to become the new stewards of the grove and to play a role in its continuing preservation.

As the most visited redwoods of the nineteenth century, Big Trees Grove played a crucial role in the growing recognition of these remarkable trees. Big Trees Grove was not just a local phenomenon. Through the simple acts of its first visitors—from having a picnic to taking a stroll through the forest— the wonder of the redwoods entered the national consciousness. This small grove of Big Trees changed history and planted the seeds of appreciation that led to all the redwood parks we enjoy today. Rediscovering and retelling the grove's resort history helps in restoring the national profile of Big Trees Grove and its place in the history of the preservation movement. Big Trees Grove is where the public got to know the redwoods and where they fell in love with them.

Appendix A

NAMED TREES AT BIG TREES GROVE

Most of the named trees were located on Welch's Big Trees Grove. When viewing trees, please stay on designated trails only and do not climb on the trees or their roots.
* Shown on the Revised Historic Redwood Loop Trail Map

Tree Name	History
Address	*see Calling Card*
Admiral Hugh Rodman	*see U.S. Navy*
Aladdin Temple	Dedicated on June 14, 1902, for the Aladdin Temple of the Ancient Arabic Order of the Nobles of the Mystic Shrine, Columbus, Ohio.
Amaranth	Dedicated on August 6, 1922. Named for the Order of the Amaranth, a Masonic-affiliated organization for Master Masons founded in 1873.
Association Group	*see YMCA*
Bear Claw*	Date of naming unknown. Currently the tallest tree in the grove at just over 275 feet. It is located behind the Visitor Center.

Tree Name	History
Bear's Den	Name applied by 1932. Two openings at the base of the tree formed a hollow that resembles a bear's den.
Bench	The tree was discovered and named by park docent Dave Kuty around 2006. A wooden plank was placed in a partial opening of the tree.
BIA	Dedicated on May 4, 1906. Named for the Boys' Industrial Association of the Anthracite Coal Region, Wyoming.
Big Shell	Name applied by 1949. Described the remains of a giant redwood with a young tree growing from its top.
Big Tree Crater	Name applied by 1932 for the depression in the ground formed by the decayed base of a large redwood.
Blaine	Origin and date of naming unknown. Possibly named in 1884 for Republican presidential nominee James G. Blaine.
Boss, The	Origin of name unknown. Possibly named by the 1880s.
Bracer, The	Name applied by 1932. Described as having grown a burl brace to an old platform and then reached down to the earth.
Bridal Chamber House	*see Fremont*
California World War I Veterans	Dedicated on May 15, 1927, to Californians who served in World War I. Located on Cowell's Big Trees. Rededicated at Cowell's Big Trees by the American Legion to honor the hero dead.
Calling Card *(aka World's Largest Calling Card Case)*	Name applied by the 1880s. Located at Big Tree Station on Cowell's Big Trees. Called the World's Largest Calling Card Case because tourists tacked personal visiting calling cards and notes on it.

Tree Name	History
Castro *(aka General Castro)*	Name applied by 1883 for José Antonio Castro, comandante general of the Mexican army in Alta California.
Cathedral or Cathedral Group	May refer to several different multi-trunk trees in the grove. *see Ingersoll's Cathedral*
Cathedral Spires	Name applied by 1904. May refer to Ingersoll's Cathedral.
Cecil B. DeMille	Named in 1916 for the famous movie director when he came to the grove to film the movie *Trail of the Lonesome Pine.*
Centennial Group	Name applied by 1889. Described as a family circle standing near the hotel with each tree named for a Revolutionary War hero: the George Washington, Thomas Jefferson, John Adams, James Monroe, Alexander Hamilton, Benjamin Franklin and Martha Washington.
Chimney	Name applied by the 1890s. The name usually describes a tree with a vertical, hollow center.
Christian Endeavor in Dixie	This possible tree name comes from a bronze plaque found in the park that may have been used as part of a tree dedication on July 13, 1925. The Christian Endeavor Society was formed in 1881 in Maine and was the first national church youth organization.
Cleveland *(aka President Cleveland)*	Name applied by 1902 for U.S. president Grover Cleveland, who served as the twenty-second (1885–89) and twenty-fourth (1893–97) president.
Cleveland Grays	Dedicated on July 12, 1912, for the independent militia company in Cleveland, Ohio, in commemoration of its seventy-fifth anniversary.
Commercial Law League of America	Named in 1915 for the attorney organization. It was described as a tree with two trunks representing the men and women of the league.
Corinthian Yacht Club	Dedicated on July 29, 1910. Named for the San Francisco club.

Tree Name	History
Corkscrews	*see Three Twisters*
Daniel Webster	Name applied in 1889 by T.H. Smith of Boston, Massachusetts, for the American statesman and orator who served as U.S. senator from 1827 to 1841 and 1845 to 1850.
Daughters of America	This possible tree name comes from a bronze plaque found in the park that may have been used as part of a tree dedication on September 13, 1931. The Daughters of America was a secret Nativist society founded in 1891 as an auxiliary of the Junior Order of the United American Mechanics.
Dog	Name applied by 1879. Apparently had a burl that resembled a dog.
Dragon	Date of naming unknown. It apparently had a burl that resembled a dragon.
Driveway	Name applied by 1906. May refer to the Natural Graft Tree.
Duane	Name applied by 1891. Origin of name unknown.
Eagle's Nest	Name applied by 1892. Origin of name unknown.
E. Clemens Horst	This possible tree name comes from a bronze plaque found in the park that may have been used as part of a tree dedication on December 25, 1914. The dedication was made by Samuel H. Cowell. Emil Clemens Horst (1867–1940) was a major figure in the cultivation, harvest and sale of hops in the United States. With an office in San Francisco, Horst owned the largest acreage of hops in the world.
Epworth League	Named in 1901 for the Methodist young adult association.
Fallen Monarch (aka *Monarch of the Forest*)	Named in 1910. A fallen Big Tree that visitors stood on for photographs.

Tree Name	History
Fallen Sister*	Originally one of the Three Sisters. This tree fell in a storm in 1915. The fire-scarred base stands among the Fremont Group.
Fernery, The	Named applied by 1889. Described the stump of a tree cut up high from the ground whose flat top was filled with ferns. The Fernery was located near the Castro Tree.
"Fighting Bob" Evans	Dedicated on May 5, 1908, for Robley Evans, the commander in chief of the U.S. Atlantic fleet known as the "Great White Fleet."
Flatiron	*see Wonder*
Fraternal Order of Eagles	Dedicated to the fraternal organization on May 20, 1909.
Fremont* *(aka General Fremont, the Pioneer, House Tree, Bridal Chamber House)*	By 1868, it began being called the Fremont Tree in honor of the explorer John Charles Frémont. A story arose that it housed Frémont during his 1846 expedition.
Fremont's Tree	*see the Giant*
Garfield *(aka President Garfield)*	Name applied by 1884 for U.S. president James Garfield, who served as the twentieth U.S. president from March 4, 1881, to September 19, 1881. He was shot by an assassin on July 2, 1881, and passed away on September 19, 1881. It is possible that this name was temporarily given to the Giant.
The Giant* *(aka Fremont's Tree [1st], San Lorenzo Giant, Rotary Tree)*	In 1846, Isaac Graham originally named it Fremont's Tree in honor of explorer John Charles Frémont. By the late 1860s, it became known as the San Lorenzo Giant or simply the Giant. It was dedicated to Rotary International in 1938.

Tree Name	History
Giant Burl* *(aka Buhrl)*	Name applied by 1889 due to the large burl that protrudes from one side. In 1939, it was described as "Nature's Trylon and Perisphere" in reference to the two monumental, modernistic structures at the 1939 New York World's Fair.
Gillespie	Named by 1902 for W.A. Gillespie, tour agent of the Pennsylvania Railroad. Others believe it was named for U.S. Marine Corps lieutenant Archibald H. Gillespie, who, as a courier, brought a secret message to John Frémont in Alta California in 1846.
Goose Pen*	Name applied by the 1950s. The burnt hollow bases of such trees were often used by early settlers as animal pens.
Governor Nash	Dedicated on May 14, 1901, in honor of Ohio governor George K. Nash.
Graffiti	A tree beginning in the 1880s upon which visitors carved their names and messages. Today, carving on trees is strictly prohibited.
Grand Army of the Republic (1st)	Dedicated on February 28, 1903, for the Grand Army of the Republic (GAR). Named in honor of Thomas J. Stewart, the U.S. representative from New York from 1867 to 1869. This GAR Tree was located on Cowell's Big Trees but was in danger of being logged.
Grand Army of the Republic (2nd)	Dedicated by 1904 at Welch's Big Trees Grove to replace the original GAR Tree.
Grand Grove of Druids	Dedicated in 1938 for the fraternal organization. Located on Cowell's Big Trees.
Grant* *(aka General Grant)*	Dedicated in 1879 for the eighteenth U.S. president, Ulysses S. Grant, who served from 1869 to 1877.
Hancock *(aka General Hancock)*	Name applied by 1892 for Union general Winfield Scott Hancock.

Tree Name	History
Harrison *(aka Harrison Group, President Harrison)*	Named by 1890 for the twenty-third U.S. president, Benjamin Harrison, who served from 1889 to 1893. Described as containing burls shaped like an Indian head and an elephant head. One account described part of the group as "his wife is quite as large as he, and little baby McKee stands close by."
Hattie	Name applied by 1885. Origin of name unknown.
Hen and Chicks	Name applied by 1932. Described as a large tree surrounded by several smaller sprouts.
House	*see Fremont*
Ida	Name applied by 1883. Origin of name unknown.
Ingersoll's Cathedral* *(aka Robert Ingersoll, Bob Ingersoll, Colonel Ingersoll)*	Multi-trunk tree named after the 1884 visit of famed American orator Robert Green Ingersoll, known as the "Great Agnostic."
James J. Jeffries	Dedicated in 1910 for American heavyweight champion (1899–1905) boxer known as the "Great White Hope."
James M. Lynch	Dedicated on August 12, 1911, for the president of the International Typographical Union.
Jeter*	Dedicated on May 12, 1934, to William T. Jeter, thirty-five-year president of Santa Cruz County Bank, mayor of Santa Cruz from 1892 to 1894 and lieutenant governor of California from 1895 to 1899. Jeter played an instrumental role in purchasing Big Trees Grove from the Welch family so it could be made into Santa Cruz County Big Trees Park in 1930. A bronze plaque once attached to the tree is now located on the ground near the tree.
J. Sterling Morton	Dedicated in 1904 for the secretary of the Department of Agriculture (1893–97) and founder of Arbor Day, which is celebrated annually on the last Friday of April.

Tree Name	History
Jumbo*	Name applied sometime after 1882 for a burl on the tree that resembled the head of Jumbo the African elephant in the London Zoo. In 1882, P.T. Barnum purchased Jumbo for his circus in the United States.
Junior Order United American Mechanics	This possible tree name comes from a bronze plaque found in the park that may have been used as part of a tree dedication on March 15, 1931. The Order of United American Mechanics, originally the Union of Workers, was an anti-Catholic American Nativist organization founded amid the anti-alien riots in Philadelphia, 1844–45.
Knights Templar	*see Pennsylvania*
Ladies' Forest and Song-Bird Protective Association	Dedicated in 1903 for the nature association. Josephine Clifford McCrackin was president of the group, which was later affiliated with the Audobon Society. Reportedly located next to the Roosevelt Tree.
Lightning	Date of naming unknown. The unusual damage and burl growth midway up the trunk was originally believed to have been caused by a lightning strike. Naturalists now dispute this theory, but the cause of the damage remains a mystery.
Lincoln *(aka President Lincoln)*	Name applied by 1905 for the sixteenth U.S. president, Abraham Lincoln, who served from 1861 to 1865 and was assassinated on April 15, 1865.
Logan *(aka General Logan)*	Name applied by 1889. Located near the General Sherman Tree and part of a group referred to as Sherman's Lieutenants.
Los Angeles Produce Exchange	Name applied by 1913 by the San Francisco Dairy and Fruit Exchange.

Tree Name	History
Mary Pickford	Named in 1917 when the actress came to the grove to film *A Romance of the Redwoods.* When she was asked to have a Big Tree named in her honor, Pickford insisted that a small redwood tree be named instead.
McKinley* *(aka President McKinley)*	Dedicated in 1901 after the twenty-fifth U.S. president, William McKinley, who served from 1897 to 1901 and was assassinated on September 14, 1901.
Monarch of the Forest	*see Fallen Monarch*
Mother and Daughter	*see Mother and Son*
Mother and Son *(aka Mother and Daughter)*	Name applied by 1932. Described two trees joined with a natural graft at 150 feet above the ground. In 1949, this tree was also referred to as the Mother and Daughter Tree.
Natural Graft* *(aka Triple Burn)*	Name applied by 1932. Describes two fire-scarred trees joined by a natural graft. It may also have been referred to as the Triple Burn Tree.
Neckbreaker*	Name applied by 1932. Describes a straight-trunk tree free of limbs for its first two hundred feet.
Nine Muses*	Name applied by 1889. Named after the Nine Muses of Greek mythology: Thalia (comedy), Urania (astronomy), Melpomene (tragedy), Polyhymnia (hymns), Erato (lyric poetry), Calliope (epic poetry), Clio (history), Euterpe (flute playing) and Terpsichore (choral lyric and dancing). It was once the site of the bandstand.
Octopus	Date of naming unknown. Original top of tree grew at an angle, and the overall tree was shaped like an octopus.
Old Glory	Name applied by 1906. The term "Old Glory" is a nickname for the flag of the United States.

Tree Name	History
Pennsylvania	Name applied by 1906. Was the only known tree in the grove named for a state. Possibly named for the Reading Commandery No. 42 Knights Templars of Pennsylvania, a Freemason organization.
Photo-op *(aka Kodak Tree, Banana Slug Hotel)*	The multiple, fused trunk tree located across from the Visitor Center. The various names were applied over the past few decades because this tree at the park entrance is a popular spot for taking photographs. Banana slugs are often seen moving in and out of an opening on the tree.
Pioneer	*see Fremont*
Professor Campbell	Name applied by 1891. Origin of name unknown.
Pythian Sisters	*see Twin Redwoods*
Roosevelt* *(aka President Roosevelt)*	Dedicated on May 11, 1903, during the visit of the twenty-sixth U.S. president, Theodore Roosevelt, who served from 1901 to 1909. A 1902 article mentioned a smaller tree previously named for Roosevelt when he was vice president.
Rotary (1st)	Dedicated on June 12, 1922, to Rotary International. The tree was described as a cathedral group.
Rotary (2nd)	*see the Giant*
Royal Neighbors of America	This possible tree name comes from a bronze plaque found in the park that may have been used as part of a tree dedication circa 1925–28. The Royal Neighbors of America was a fraternal benefit society founded by women in 1895. It was the first organization to offer women life insurance.
Saddle	Date of naming unknown. Once had a low branch shaped like a horse saddle.

Tree Name	History
Sam Houston	Named in 1902 for the president of the Republic of Texas from 1836 to 1838 and 1841 to 1844.
San Lorenzo Giant	*see the Giant*
Seven Sisters	Name applied by 1892. Likely named for the Seven Stars of the Pleiades constellation from Greek mythology: Maia, Alcyone, Electra, Celaeno, Taygeta, Asterope and Merope.
Sheridan *(aka General Sheridan)*	Name applied by 1889. Located near the General Sherman Tree and part of a group referred to as Sherman's Lieutenants.
Sherman* *(aka General Sherman)*	Dedicated in 1881 for Union general William Tecumseh Sherman.
Sunday School Association	*see YMCA*
Taft (?)	It is uncertain if a tree was ever officially named for the twenty-seventh U.S. president, William Howard Taft, who served from 1909 to 1913.
Thomas J. Stewart	*see Grand Army of the Republic (1ˢᵗ)*
Three Graces	Name applied by 1917. Named for the Greek goddesses—Thalia (good cheer), Aglaia (splendor) and Euphrosyne (mirth)—representing the attributes of joy, charm and beauty.
Three Sisters*	Name applied by 1883. Describes three trees with connected roots and includes the Fallen Sister, which fell during a storm in 1915. Located in the Fremont Group.
Three Twisters *(aka Corkscrews)*	Name applied by 1932. Named for how the bark twists around their trunks.
Triple Burn	*see Natural Graft*
Tunnel	Date of naming unknown. It is assumed that this tree was hollowed in some fashion. May refer to a tree with a low tunnel located outside the Redwood Loop Trail.

Tree Name	History
Twelve Apostles	Name applied by 1904 for the twelve apostles: Peter, Andrew, James, John, Philip, Bartholomew, Thomas, Matthew, James the Younger, Judas, Jude and Simon. This tree might also be the one more widely known as Ingersoll's Cathedral.
Twin	Name applied by 1932. Two trees of similar size adjoining each other. Was noted on a park brochure as being at a different location than the Twin Redwoods.
Twin Redwoods	The name Twin Sisters was applied by 1889 and Pythian Sisters (auxiliary of the Knights of Phythias) applied in 1927. Describes two trees of the same size joined at the root and forming a partial room. Often depicted in postcards with a wooden floor between the trees. May have described part of the Three Sisters.
Twin Sisters	*see Twin Redwoods*
Undercut	Name applied by the 1930s. It is believed that early loggers began cutting the tree but stopped partway, leaving a scar.
United States Navy* *(aka Admiral Hugh Rodman, U.S. Pacific Fleet)*	Dedicated on August 26, 1919, to the officers and men of the U.S. Pacific Fleet: Admiral Hugh Rodman, commander-in-chief. Commemorated the fleet's crossing of the Panama Canal.
U.S. Pacific Fleet	*see U.S. Navy*
Veterans	*see California World War I Veterans*
Welded	Date of naming unknown. Apparently described at least two trees that grew together.
William Jennings Bryan	Name applied by 1902 for the American orator William Jennings Bryan. This tree may be the same as the Fallen Sister, which fell in 1915.
Woman's Benefit Association	Originally dedicated in 1927. Rededicated in 1937.

Tree Name	History
Wonder* *(aka Wonder Group, Flatiron)*	Name applied by 1932. This tree exhibits reiteration, meaning that branches grow parallel to the trunk, repeating the trunk shape and appearing as upturned fingers on a hand.
YMCA Young Men's Christian Association* *(aka Association Group, Sunday School Association)*	Dedicated on May 17, 1887. The same tree was dedicated on June 28, 1911, for the Sunday School Workers of North America.

SILENT MOVIES FILMED AT BIG TREES GROVE

1911

A Diamond in the Rough
Director: Francis Boggs
Starring: Sidney Ayres, Bessie Eyton, George Hernandez, Herbert Rawlinson, Fred Huntley (note: George Hernandez grew up in Watsonville)
Storyline: A mountain girl, engaged to a woodsman selected by her father, rescues a lost tourist, and romance ensues. (This movie features Harry Cowell's favorite ox team.)

1915

The Primal Lure
Director: William S. Hart
Starring: William S. Hart, Margery Wilson, Robert McKim
Storyline: The manager of a remote Canadian trading post overcomes romantic difficulties, a villain and a band of hostile Indians.

1916

Trail of the Lonesome Pine
Director: Cecil B. DeMille
Starring: Charlotte Walker, Thomas Meighan, Theodore Roberts, Earle Foxe
Storyline: A gang of moonshiners is tracked down by a federal agent, assisted by the ringleader's daughter. (The lonesome pine is played by a redwood.)

1917

Freckles
Director: Marshall Neilan
Starring: Jack Pickford, Louise Huff, Hobart Bosworth
Storyline: A one-armed orphan wins the love of a pretty girl when he saves her from a falling tree.

A Romance of the Redwoods
Director: Cecil B. DeMille
Starring: Mary Pickford, Elliot Dexter
Storyline: An orphaned girl comes to California during the gold rush to live with her uncle but discovers he is dead and that his identity has been stolen by an outlaw.

1918

"Blue Blazes" Rawden
Director: William S. Hart
Starring: William S. Hart, Maud George, Gertrude Claire, Robert McKim, Jack Hoxie
Storyline: A lumber boss wins a dance hall and a mistress in a deadly duel but suffers the consequences when his rival's family arrives on the scene.

1919

False Evidence
Director: Edwin Carewe
Starring: Viola Dana, Wheeler Oakman
Storyline: A lumberman's daughter, betrothed to a bully, stabs him. Her true lover is accused of the crime, but she saves him from a lynch mob.

1920

Jes' Call Me Jim
Director: Clarence G. Badger
Starring: Will Rogers, Irene Rich, Jimmy Rogers
Storyline: The hero helps rescue a falsely imprisoned inventor and punishes the man who stole his invention and his freedom.

The Testing Block
Director: Lambert Hillyer
Starring: William S. Hart, Eva Novak
Storyline: An outlaw, hiding in the redwoods, fights his gang for the hand of the heroine before marrying her at gunpoint. The birth of their child leads to his redemption.

1923

Eyes of the Forest
Director: Lambert Hillyer
Starring: Tom Mix, Pauline Starke, Sid Jordan
Storyline: A forest ranger rescues the heroine from a murder charge by tracking down the real villain from the air.

1924

The Last Man on Earth
Director: John Blystone
Starring: Earle Foxe, Grace Cunard, Gladys Tennyson

Storyline: An epidemic kills off all virile men except for one hermit. When he is discovered living in the Fremont Tree, every woman on the planet wants him.

The Man Who Fights Alone
Director: Wallace Worsley
Starring: William Farnum, Lois Wilson, Edward Everett Horton
Storyline: A wheelchair-bound husband contemplates suicide when he suspects his wife of cheating, but fate forces him to become a hero.

1926

Phantom of the Forest
Director: Henry McCarty
Starring: Thunder (dog), White Fawn (dog), Betty Francisco, Eddie Phillips
Storyline: A lost puppy that grows up smart and strong in the redwoods saves a young woman from foreclosure and rescues a baby from a forest fire.

Compiled by Traci Bliss and Randall Brown

NOTES

In the Beginning

1. The full name of Mission Santa Cruz is Misión la exaltación de la Santa Cruz. A circa 1820s portion of the mission's housing, built by and lived in by Native people, is preserved as part of Santa Cruz Mission State Historic Park.
2. Rizzo, "Indigenous Justice or Padre Killers?," 12.
3. Clarke, *Untold History*.
4. Hylkema, "Native American Cultural Landscape," 23.
5. Cuthrell, "Quiroste Valley Cultural Preserve."
6. The full title of Rancho Rincon is Rancho Cañada del Rincon en el Rio San Lorenzo.
7. José Guillermo Bocle, who apparently had many aliases, eventually became known as William Thompson.
8. There is no documentation on whether the term Drunkards Camp was ever used historically to describe the Zayante settlement. The name Roaring Camp was bestowed in 1963 to the privately owned railroad attraction located next to the park.
9. "Death of a Pioneer," *Santa Cruz Weekly Sentinel*, 2:1. Joseph Majors married Marie de los Angele Castro at Mission Santa Cruz in 1839.
10. Bartleson, "Oregon and California," 1:5–6. The United States Regiment of Dragoons was organized in 1833. Its designation was changed to the First Regiment of Cavalry by the act of August 3, 1861.

Chapter 1

11. Denton, "Frémont Steals California," 2.

12. Frémont, *Memoirs of My Life*, 457.

13. Brown and Bliss, "Two Trees for General Fremont," 102.

14. Patten, "Loss of Historical Aspects," 18:5–8.

15. Brown and Bliss, "Two Trees for General Fremont," 103–4.

16. Denton, "Frémont Steals California," 3.

17. Breckenridge, *Thomas E. Breckenridge Memoirs*, 56.

18. Lewis, "John C. Fremont."

19. Denton, "Frémont Steals California," 4.

20. The United States declared war on Mexico on May 13, 1846.

21. Beck and Hasse, "Bear Flag Revolt."

22. Phillips, "Town of Mariposa."

23. "What Is a Name: The Golden Gate?" Frémont's inspiration for the name Golden Gate came from the Byzantine harbor Chrysoceras, also known as the Golden Horn.

24. The name *ho-o-pe*, meaning "red pine tree" in the Awaswas dialect, was provided by California State Park archaeologist Mark Hylkema. On October 10, 1769, near the present-day town of Watsonville, Father Juan Crespi recorded in his journal the name *palo colorado* for the newly discovered trees.

25. "Lofty Trees," *Aurora of the Valley*, 1:4–5. Karl Friedrich Hieronymus was Baron Munchausen, a German storyteller whose tall tales were the basis of a book by Rudolf Erich Raspe in 1785.

26. "Fremont's Saplings," *Santa Cruz Weekly Sentinel*, 3:2.

27. "Sayante Valley," *Sacramento Daily Union*, 2:4.

28. Vischer, *Vischer's Pictorial*, 58.

29. Palmquist and Kailbourn, *Pioneeer Photographers*, 571.

30. "Curiosities of Santa Cruz," *Santa Cruz Weekly Sentinel*, 2:3.

31. Vischer, *Vischer's Pictorial*, 58.

32. "Curiosities of Santa Cruz," *Santa Cruz Weekly Sentinel*, 2:3. It is believed that several fires over the past three hundred years may have created and widened the entrance to the Fremont Tree.

33. "Notes of a Trip of the S.F.B.D. Agricultural Society," 1:2.

34. "Notes of a Trip to the Zayante," *Santa Cruz County Times*, 2:2.

35. Goode, "Pretty Obstinate Set of Fellows," 33.

36. Robinson, "San Lorenzo Valley Flume Chronicle," 51.

37. "Trip to Felton," *Santa Cruz Sentinel*, 1:6.

38. Vessey, "Economy of the Vegetable Kingdom," 153:1.

39. Greene, "Big Trees of California," 18.

40. Wilson, "Decoding the Redwoods."

41. Piwarzyk and Miller, *Valley of Redwoods*, 30–31.
42. Perry et al., *Lime Kiln Legacies*, 48.
43. MacDougall, "Henry Cowell and His Family," 3–6.
44. Perry, "Who Was Henry Cowell?"
45. "Millionaire Cowell," *Santa Cruz Sentinel*, 4:1. It must be noted that a July 17, 1902 *Santa Cruz Sentinel* article stated that Henry Cowell gave a $1,000 donation (equivalent to $30,000 today) to the Home for Incurables in San Francisco. Henry Cowell's descendants were noted philanthropists. His children Samuel H., Isabella and Helen built Blindcraft, which later became Lighthouse for the Blind in 1924.
46. Piwarzyk and Miller, *Valley of Redwoods*, 32.
47. On April 5, 1972, the S.H. Cowell Foundation gift-deeded 2,335 acres of forestland to the State of California, creating the Fall Creek unit of the park. In 1988, an additional 30 acres were donated by Goldie Agner Barr.
48. "Santa Cruz Big Trees Said to Be in Danger," *Santa Cruz Evening Sentinel*, 4:3.

Chapter 2

49. "Fire in the Mountains," *Daily Evening Herald*, 1:4.
50. This story was related to the author by Jim Kliment. The story was first related by Margaret Welch Coolidge, wife of Stanly Welch, to Norman Clark, founder of Roaring Camp Railroads.
51. "Real Estate Transactions," *Santa Cruz Weekly Sentinel*, 2:4. The transaction included portions of Ranchos Sayante and Rincon.
52. This story was related to the author by Jim Kliment. The story was first related by Margaret Welch Coolidge, wife of Stanly Welch, to Norman Clark, founder of Roaring Camp Railroads.
53. Jeter, "Welch Big Tree Grove," July 18, 1928, 3:2–4. This article states that Joseph Warren Welch traveled back to Massachusetts to marry Anna Isabella Learned. Anna's 1905 obituary claims she came to California via the Isthmus of Panama in 1849. The Rhode Island Marriage Index, 1851–1920, lists a marriage of a Joseph W. Welch Jr. and Anna J. Leonard on August 13, 1852.
54. "Pacific Coast Items," *Sacramento Daily Union*, 1:3.
55. "California Great Registers," Joseph Warren Welch, 24 Jul 1866; citing Voter Registration, 434 Fremont, San Francisco, California, United States, county clerk offices, California; FHL microfilm 977,097.
56. This story was related to the author by Jim Kliment. The story was first related by Margaret Welch Coolidge, wife of Stanly Welch, to Norman Clark, founder of Roaring Camp Railroads.
57. "Santa Cruz Jubilant," *San Francisco Chronicle*, 3:3.
58. Nash, *Wilderness and the American Mind*, 67–75.
59. "Fremont's Saplings," *Santa Cruz Weekly Sentinel*, 3:2.

60. Worth, "59 of '86 Letters Written," 48–49.
61. Robinson, *San Lorenzo Valley*, 17.
62. "Santa Cruz," *Santa Cruz Sentinel*, 1:4.
63. Casey, "End of the Line."
64. "Fremont's Saplings," *Santa Cruz Weekly Sentinel*, 3:2.
65. The 1955 flood took out the last swinging bridge over the San Lorenzo River.
66. Howard, *Howard of Glossop's Journal of a Tour*, 76–79.
67. *Santa Cruz Weekly Sentinel*, May 4, 1878, 3:2.
68. Otto, "Old Santa Cruz," 11:7.
69. "Fremont's Saplings," *Santa Cruz Weekly Sentinel*, 3:2.
70. "Big Trees," *Santa Cruz Daily Surf*, June 8, 1889, 2:1–2. Idlewild Glade was likely used for camping by early visitors.
71. Beal and Beal, *Santa Cruz Beach Boardwalk*, 15.
72. Ibid., 34–39.
73. "House in California One Thousand Years Old," *Vermont Phœnix*, 4:3.
74. Ibid.
75. Willey, *Santa Cruz County*, 30.
76. "What They Saw," *Santa Cruz Weekly Sentinel*, 3:4.
77. Information obtained from Lisa Robinson, director of the San Lorenzo Valley Historical Society.

Chapter 3

78. Hamman, *California Central Coast Railways*, 83–84.
79. Gordon, "Down the Coast," 1:4.
80. "Santa Cruz Jubilant," *San Francisco Chronicle*, 3:3.
81. Gordon, "Down the Coast," 1:4.
82. "Selfish Policy," *Santa Cruz Weekly Sentinel*, 2:1.
83. Whaley, "Railroads." Additional information obtained from Jim Kliment.

Chapter 4

84. *Santa Cruz Weekly Sentinel*, November 20, 1875, 3:1.
85. The first name of I. Douglas Welch is not recorded. It might have been Isaac since that was the name of Anna's father.
86. "Pacific Coast Items," *Sacramento Daily Union*, 1:3.
87. "Santa Cruz Letter," *Santa Cruz Weekly Sentinel*, 2:2–3.
88. "Felton Items," *Santa Cruz Weekly Sentinel*, September 23, 1876, 3:3.
89. *Santa Cruz Weekly Sentinel*, August 18, 1877, 2:9.
90. "Summer Recreation in the Open Air," *Santa Cruz Weekly Sentinel*, 3:2.

91. "Santa Cruz Letter," *Santa Cruz Weekly Sentinel*, 2:2–3.

92. "Gala Day," *Santa Cruz Weekly Sentinel*, 3:4.

93. "The Santa Cruz Big Trees," *Santa Cruz Courier*, April 26, 1877.

94. Hoitt, *Pacific Coast Guide*, 113.

95. "Social and Personal," *Santa Cruz Sentinel*, 3:3.

96. "Episcopal Church Picnic," *Santa Cruz Weekly Sentinel*, 3:5.

97. "Santa Cruz Letter," *Santa Cruz Weekly Sentinel*, 2:2–3.

98. *Santa Cruz Weekly Sentinel*, May 12, 1877, 3:3.

99. *Santa Cruz Weekly Sentinel*, August 18, 1877, 2:9.

100. *Santa Cruz Weekly Sentinel*, May 12, 1877, 3:3.

101. *Santa Cruz Weekly Sentinel*, May 19, 1877, 2:5.

102. *Santa Cruz Weekly Sentinel*, May 26, 1877, 3:2.

103. *Santa Cruz Weekly Sentinel*, May 12, 1877, 3:3.

104. Brown, *Trees with Names*, 4.

105. Heath, "At a Watering Place," 2:5.

106. State of California, *Appendix to the Journals of the Senate and Assembly of the Twenty-Seventh Session*, 1887, 283.

107. Heath, "At a Watering Place," 2:5.

108. Jepson, *Jepson Field Book*, 180.

109. "Mammoth Trees," *Santa Cruz Weekly Sentinel*, 2:3.

110. State of California, *Appendix to the Journals of the Senate and Assembly of the Twenty-Seventh Session*, 1887, 283.

111. "The Big Trees," *Santa Cruz Daily Surf*, October 9, 1884, 2:2.

112. "What They Saw," *Santa Cruz Weekly Sentinel*, 3:4.

113. Vischer, *Vischer's Pictorial*, 58.

114. "Missourian's View of the 'Golden West,'" *Lexington Intelligencer*, 1:6.

115. Hardy, *Through Cities and Prairie Lands*, 256.

116. "Big Trees," *Santa Cruz Daily Surf*, 2:1. Perhaps the stovepipe hole was large enough to also serve as a source of light.

117. *Santa Cruz Weekly Sentinel*, May 19, 1877, 2:5.

118. *Santa Cruz Weekly Sentinel*, May 4, 1878, 3:3.

119. "At the Big Trees," *Santa Cruz Weekly Sentinel*, 2:2.

120. *Santa Cruz Weekly Sentinel*, July 29, 1882, 2:4.

121. "Episcopal Church Picnic," *Santa Cruz Weekly Sentinel*, 3:5.

122. "Santa Cruz Letter," *Santa Cruz Weekly Sentinel*, 2:2–3.

123. *Santa Cruz Weekly Sentinel*, October 8, 1881, 3:4.

Chapter 5

124. South Pacific Coast Railroad advertisement.

125. Masters, "Horrors of the Summit Tunnel," December 8, 2014.

126. Perry et al., *Lime Kiln Legacies*, 131.
127. "Workingmen's Picnic," *Santa Cruz Weekly Sentinel*, 3:5–6. A notable exception to the general treatment of the Chinese during this period was the operation of a Chinese mission by the Santa Cruz Congregational Church from 1881 until 1920.
128. "Santa Cruz Letter," *Santa Cruz Weekly Sentinel*, 2:2–3. Unfortunately, a search of the Chinese immigration case files at the National Archives at San Francisco did not reveal any documents or further information on the life of Quong Long Sing.
129. "Felton Items," *Santa Cruz Weekly Sentinel*, 3:6.
130. Colegrove, *Life Story of George L. Colegrove*, 113.
131. "South Pacific Coast Railroad," *Santa Cruz Weekly Sentinel*, 2:3.
132. "Santa Cruz Letter," *Santa Cruz Weekly Sentinel*, 2:2–3.
133. "S.P.C.R.R.," *Santa Cruz Weekly Sentinel*, 3:5–6.
134. Clifford, *From Geyser to Canon*, 114.
135. "S.P.C.R.R.," *Santa Cruz Weekly Sentinel*, 3:5–6.
136. Ryland, "Missourian's Letter," 2:1.
137. South Pacific Coast Railroad advertisement.

Chapter 6

138. *Santa Cruz Weekly Sentinel*, May 27, 1882, 2:1.
139. Manna and Van Zant, *Brands of Calaveras County*, 122.
140. "Latest Camp," *Santa Cruz Daily Surf*, 3:4.
141. "Felton Letter," *Santa Cruz Weekly Sentinel*, June 12, 1880, 2:3.
142. Griswold, *Beauties of California*.
143. Harrison, *History of Santa Cruz County*, 216.
144. "Annual High Jinks," *Santa Cruz Sentinel*, 3:3.
145. Reader, *To Know My Name*, 15–19.
146. "Annual High Jinks," *Santa Cruz Sentinel*, 3:3.
147. "Bangos," *Santa Cruz Sentinel*, 3:6.
148. "Tough Crowd," *Santa Cruz Sentinel*, 1:7.
149. *Santa Cruz Weekly Sentinel*, July 29, 1882, 2:4.
150. Nash, *Wilderness and the American Mind*, 125.
151. "California in Retrospect," *Orleans County Monitor*, 1:3.
152. Erk, "Merry Crusade to the Golden Gate," 203.
153. Bliss and Brown. "Celebrity Visitors," 113.
154. *Santa Cruz Sentinel*, October 1, 1884, 3:1.
155. Barber, "Ingersoll's Cathedral," 154.
156. Nye, "Under the Big Trees," 14:3.
157. Leek, "Our California Letter," 1:7.
158. Barber, "Ingersoll's Cathedral," 154.
159. Clinton, "California Giant," 35:7.

Chapter 7

160. Tweed, *King Sequoia*, 16.

161. Ibid., 33.

162. "Curiosities," *Santa Cruz Weekly Sentinel*, 2:3.

163. Tweed, *King Sequoia*, 33.

164. Ibid., 94–95. The Pioneer Tree fell during a storm on January 8, 2017. The Wawona Tree fell during a snowstorm in 1969.

165. "Felton Big Tree Grove," *Santa Cruz Sentinel*, 1:3.

166. "Santa Cruz Big Trees," *Santa Cruz Sentinel*, 2:4.

167. Raymond, *Santa Cruz County*, 50.

168. "Felton," *Santa Cruz Sentinel*, 3:3.

169. *California Guide for Tourists and Settlers*, 35.

170. Curtis, "Trees of Santa Cruz," 12:2. General Grant National Park became known as Kings Canyon National Park in 1940. Today, it is part of Sequoia–Kings Canyon National Parks.

171. "Visit of a Renowned Botanist," *Santa Cruz Weekly Sentinel*, 2:3.

172. Jepson, *Jepson Field Book*, 180.

173. Muir, letter to Jeanne C. Carr. The John Muir Drawings collection at the same institution also includes a drawing of redwoods by Muir titled *Redwood near Santa Cruz. Fired and Renewed.*

174. Filmer, "Decoding the Redwoods." DNA is deoxyribonucleic acid, which is a self-replicating material in chromosomes that carries genetic information.

175. Cook, *Giant Sequoias of California*. A third sequoia known as the Dawn redwood (*Metasequoia glyptostroboides*), once thought extinct, was discovered in the 1940s in the mountains of China. The much smaller tree also differs from the others in its genus, being the only one that is deciduous.

176. "Big Trees," *Santa Cruz Daily Surf*, October 9, 1884, 2:2.

177. Tweed, *King Sequoia*, 52.

178. "Big Trees," *Santa Cruz Daily Surf*, June 8, 1889, 2:1–2.

179. Tweed, *King Sequoia*, 132.

180. "Big Trees," *Santa Cruz Daily Surf.*

181. "Redwood Burl," National Park Service. The removal of burl damages the tree and can lead to the tree's death. It is illegal to harvest redwood burl in Redwood State and National Parks.

182. Perry, "Dissecting 'Jumbo,'" 1. At some point, the trunk-shaped burl broke off, and the resemblance to Jumbo faded.

183. Chase, *California Coast Trails*, 228.

Chapter 8

184. *Santa Cruz Sentinel*, April 4, 1885, 3:1.

185. Whaley, *Santa Cruz Trains*, 95.

186. *Santa Cruz Sentinel*, May 7, 1886, 3:2.

187. "Big Trees," *Santa Cruz Daily Surf*, June 8, 1889, 2:1–2.

188. "Big Tree Grove Hotel," *Santa Cruz Sentinel*, 4:4.

189. "Felton Items," *Santa Cruz Sentinel*, 2:3.

190. "California—Monterey, Santa Cruz, and the Big Trees," *Westfield Republican*, 2:4.

191. Rideout, *Camping Out in California*, 175–76. The lady may have been describing the tree known as the Nine Muses.

192. Otto, "Old Santa Cruz," 11:7. A storm in 1915 may have brought down the tree. A story that the Fallen Sister was felled by the San Francisco earthquake in 1906 is probably just that—a story. The outdoor bar was reportedly most often used to dispense ice cream rather than alcohol.

193. "Big Trees—Endeavorers Will Be Admitted," *Santa Cruz Daily Sentinel*, 1:2.

194. *Santa Cruz Sentinel*, August 5, 1893, 3:3.

195. *Santa Cruz Sentinel*, February 23, 1897, 2:2.

196. "Railroad Picnic," *Daily Alta California*, 1:3.

197. "Felton Items," *Santa Cruz Sentinel*, 2:4.

198. *Santa Cruz Sentinel*, March 28, 1891, 3:2.

199. *Santa Cruz Sentinel*, March 13, 1900, 2:2.

200. Miles, "Santa Cruz," 1:7.

201. Harrison, *History of Santa Cruz County*, 162.

202. "Santa Cruz Big Trees: Peculiarities of Their Growth," *San Francisco Chronicle*, 2.

203. "Pleasure Trip," *Santa Cruz Sentinel*, 5:5.

204. "Busch Party," *Santa Cruz Sentinel*, 4:4.

205. McCrackin, "'New' Santa Cruz," 4:1.

206. Raymond, *Santa Cruz County*, 29.

207. *Santa Cruz Sentinel*, June 1, 1892, 3:1.

208. Bliss and Brown, "Celebrity Visitors," 113. The Prince of Siam later became King Rama VI (1910–25).

209. *Santa Cruz Sentinel*, June 23, 1886, 3:3.

210. Colegrove, *Life Story of George L. Colegrove*, 132.

211. "Big Trees," *Santa Cruz Daily Surf*, October 9, 1884, 2:2.

212. "Big Trees," *Santa Cruz Daily Surf*, June 8, 1889, 2:1–2. Today, the Giant measures just over 275 feet in height. Though the Giant is still considered the grove's largest overall tree, currently the tallest tree in the grove is the Bear Claw located directly behind the Visitor Center.

213. "General Fremont," *Daily Intelligencer*, 1:2.

214. Brown and Bliss, "Two Trees for General Fremont," 108.

215. "Fremont Reception," *Santa Cruz Sentinel*, 3:2.

216. Ibid.

217. "Pathfinder: General Fremont," *San Francisco Examiner*, 4:7.

218. "Fremont Coming Home," *Los Angeles Herald*, 1:6.

219. "Fremont Reception," *Santa Cruz Sentinel*, 3:2.

220. "At the Big Trees—Reception," *Santa Cruz Daily Surf*, 4:5.

221. "Fremont Reception," *Santa Cruz Sentinel*, 3:2.

222. "At the Big Trees," *Santa Cruz Daily Surf*, 4:5.

223. "At Headquarters," *Santa Cruz Sentinel*, 3:3.

224. "Delighted Artist," *Santa Cruz Sentinel*, 3:4.

225. *Santa Cruz Sentinel*, June 25, 1889, 3:1. The South Pacific Coast Railroad was fully purchased by the Southern Pacific Railroad in 1937.

226. "Railroad Picnic," *Santa Cruz Daily Surf*, 3:5.

227. "Railroad Picnic," *Santa Cruz Sentinel*, 3:5.

228. Ibid. The thimble-rig game is otherwise known as the shell game, in which a ball is hidden under one of three containers.

229. "Felton Big Tree Grove," *Santa Cruz Sentinel*, 1:3.

230. "Greeting," *Santa Cruz Daily Surf*, 3:5.

231. "President with a Party of Distinguished Guests Hon," *Santa Cruz Daily Surf*, 3:3–5.

232. "Felton Big Tree Grove," *Santa Cruz Sentinel*, 1:3.

233. *Santa Cruz Sentinel*, May 5, 1891, 3:2.

Chapter 9

234. "Jos. Ball's Statement," *Santa Cruz Sentinel*, 3:3.

235. *Santa Cruz Sentinel*, August 13, 1891, 2:1.

236. "Big Trees for the People," *Santa Cruz Evening News*, 2:3.

237. Phillips, *Abroad and at Home*, 215–16.

238. "Felton and Ben Lomand," *Santa Cruz Daily Surf*, 1:2.

239. "Jos. Ball's Statement," *Santa Cruz Sentinel*, 3:3.

240. "Local News," *Santa Cruz Sentinel*, August 3, 1904, 3:1.

241. *Santa Cruz Sentinel*, May 2, 1891, 2:1.

242. *Santa Cruz Evening Sentinel*, April 24, 1900, 3:1.

243. "Died Suddenly," *Santa Cruz Sentinel*, 3:2.

244. McPherson, "Big Tree Outrage," 2:1.

245. *Santa Cruz Evening Sentinel*, May 30, 1902, 3.

246. "Passing Away of Mrs. Welch," *Santa Cruz Morning Sentinel*, 1:2.

247. McPherson, "Big Tree Outrage," 2:1.

248. This story was related to the author by Jim Kliment. The story was first related by Margaret Welch Coolidge, wife of Stanly Welch, to Norman Clark, founder of Roaring Camp Railroads.

249. "Local News," *Santa Cruz Sentinel*, January 25, 1905, 3:2. It is believed that Isabella and Joseph Jr. never married.
250. "Santa Cruz Group Has 6 Months," *Santa Cruz Evening News*, 3:2.
251. "Burned in Effigy," *Santa Cruz Evening News*, 1:6–7.
252. Erk, "Merry Crusade to the Golden Gate," 202.
253. Koch and Wharton, *California*, 164–67.
254. Garvin, *Grizzly Bear*, 6.
255. Clifford, *From Geyser to Canon with Mary*, 115.
256. "Big Trees Guide Is Dead," *Santa Cruz Evening News*, 2:1.
257. *Santa Cruz Sentinel*, September 17, 1907, 10:5.
258. "Locates Redwood Burl," *Santa Cruz Evening News*, 6:3.
259. *Santa Cruz Sentinel*, July 17, 1909, 1:6.
260. "Henry Staley," *Santa Cruz Evening News*, 1:3.
261. "Inside and Outside by Brent," *Santa Cruz Evening News*, 1:1. Luther Burbank was a world-renowned horticulturalist.
262. "Big Trees Guide Is Critically Ill," *Santa Cruz Sentinel*, 1:5.
263. "We Did Our Best," *Santa Cruz Daily Surf*, 1:1–5.
264. "Santa Cruz Entertains," *San Francisco Chronicle*, 3:1–4.
265. McPherson, "Artistic Souvenir," 2:1. This painting now resides with the Native Sons of the Golden West in Napa, California.

Chapter 10

266. "Millionaire Cowell," *Santa Cruz Sentinel*, 4.
267. "Cowell Dies," *San Francisco Chronicle*, 12:5.
268. "Miscellaneous," *Santa Cruz Sentinel*, 3:3.
269. Armstrong, *Sinaites*, 135.
270. "Santa Cruz Yesterdays," *Santa Cruz Sentinel*, 4:4–7.
271. Koch, "Talley-ho Trip," 8:1.
272. "San Lorenzo Valley Items," *Santa Cruz Sentinel*, 3:4.
273. "English Picnic, Etc.," *Santa Cruz Sentinel*, 2:3.
274. Robinson, "Hopkins' Big Trees."
275. "Big Trees," *Tennessean*, 2:4.
276. Willey, *Santa Cruz County*, 57.
277. Ohlenkamp, "Tells of Choir's Excursion," 5:4.
278. "Hawaiian Singers," *Santa Cruz Weekly Sentinel*, 3:4. Hawaiian musicians were booked to perform at the Casino in the summer of 1905.
279. MacFadden, *Rambles in the Far West*, 124. In the summer of 1905, the Hawaiian Sextette and the Royal Hawaiian Sextette both performed at the Santa Cruz Boardwalk.
280. Koch, "Talley-ho Trip," 8:1.
281. "M.C. Hopkins' Narrow Escape," *Santa Cruz Sentinel*, 3:2.

Chapter 11

282. *Six and a Half Tenderfeet*, 10–11.
283. Greene, "Big Trees of California," 18.
284. "Picked Up on Pacific Avenue," *Santa Cruz Daily Surf*, 1:1.
285. Bliss and Brown, "Saving Big Basin," 118.
286. "Summer Recreation in the Open Air," *Santa Cruz Weekly Sentinel*, 3:2.
287. Holder, "How a Forest Fire Was Extinguished with Wine," 346.
288. McCrackin's home, called Monte Paxaiso, was located in the Santa Cruz Mountains above Los Gatos approximately three miles southeast of the town of Wrights.
289. Holder, "How a Forest Fire Was Extinguished with Wine," 346. Bacchus was the Roman god of wine and winemaking.
290. Ibid., 339.
291. Bliss and Brown, "Which Welch?," 129.
292. *Santa Cruz Evening Sentinel*, March 28, 1901, 2:2.
293. *Santa Cruz Sentinel*, March 10, 1900, 2:4.
294. "Santa Cruz Big Trees Said to Be in Danger," *Santa Cruz Morning Sentinel*, 4:3.
295. Bliss and Brown, "Saving Big Basin," 117–18.

Chapter 12

296. Epting, *Teddy Roosevelt in California*, 10.
297. Address of President Roosevelt at Santa Cruz.
298. "President's Day in Santa Cruz," *Santa Cruz Daily Surf*, 1:1–6.
299. Ibid. An article in the *Deseret Evening News* of May 12, 1903, listed her name as Mrs. J.M. Geselterez, who resided near Watsonville.
300. "Visit of President Roosevelt," *Santa Cruz Sentinel*, 1:5.
301. "President's Visit," *Mountain Echo*, 2:1–4.
302. *Remarks of President Roosevelt at the Big Tree Grove*.
303. "Visit of President Roosevelt," *Santa Cruz Sentinel*, 1:3–6.
304. "President's Visit," *Mountain Echo*, 2:1–4.
305. A poor-quality reproduction of this image is included in the Robert Lee Dunn article titled "Roosevelt-Democrat" in *Success Magazine*, July 1907.
306. "President's Visit," *Mountain Echo*, 2:1–4.
307. "In the Midst of Tall Timber," *Deseret Evening News*, 9:5.
308. Dunn, "Roosevelt-Democrat," 510.
309. "President's Day in Santa Cruz," *Santa Cruz Surf*, 1:1–6.
310. "Memorial Gift from Nebraska," *San Francisco Call*, 3:6.

Chapter 13

311. "Dance Under the Big Trees," *San Francisco Call*, 4:5.
312. McKinley, "Cruise of the Great White Fleet."
313. Price, "Fifteen Hundred Bluejackets," 2:2–3.
314. Vandervort, "California Epistle," 1:6.
315. "You Are Immense," *San Francisco Call*, 5:2.
316. Price, "Fifteen Hundred Bluejackets," 2.
317. "Seaside and Mountain," *Arizona Republic*, 12:2.
318. Porter, "Naval History Made," 1:1.
319. "Under the Big Redwood Trees," *Midland Journal*, 2.
320. M'Isaac, "Invitation to President Taft," 5:5.
321. "Local and Personal," *North Platte Semi-Weekly Tribune*, 5:2.
322. Koch, "He Sailed into Town," 22:1.
323. Porter, "Naval History Made," 1:1.
324. "Forest Giant Bears Tablet," *Santa Cruz Evening News*, 4:2.

Chapter 14

325. "Charity Does Harm," *San Francisco Call*, 10:1.
326. "A Big Man Among the Big Trees," *Santa Cruz Sentinel*, 1:5.
327. "Charity Does Harm," *San Francisco Call*, 10:3.
328. McCrackin, "Carnegie Entertained," 2:5.
329. "Big Man Among the Big Trees," *Santa Cruz Sentinel*, 1:5. This article provides a different version of Carnegie's quote about President Roosevelt: "Roosevelt is just as straight a man as that tree is a straight tree; there is no sham about him. He is the most phenomenal man in the world today."
330. Ibid. It is believed that the redwood seedlings gifted to Carnegie did not survive since the Skibo Castle Garden plant list does not contain coast redwoods but only giant sequoias.
331. Ibid. The photograph taken of Carnegie and his party has not been located.
332. "Carnegies Visit Santa Cruz," *Impulse*, 21.

Chapter 15

333. *Santa Cruz Sentinel*, July 29, 1902, 2:4.
334. "Hopkins' Big Tree Grove," *San Francisco Chronicle*, 34:5.
335. "Gustav Rohrer, Known Here, Dies," *Santa Cruz Sentinel*, 8:1.
336. "Your Vacation Is Not Complete," *Santa Cruz Evening News*, 7:5.
337. Huxsaw, "California Big Trees Visited," 8:3–4.

338. "Historic Resources of Big Basin Redwoods State Park," National Park Service, 3–4. Big Basin now encompasses 18,130 acres.

339. "James Jackson Jeffries," Enclyclopaedia Britannica.

340. "Undefeated Champion," *San Francisco Call*, 10:2.

341. "Sing, O, Redwoods," *Santa Cruz Evening News*, 3:1–2.

342. "James Jackson Jeffries," Enclyclopaedia Britannica.

343. "Axmen Spared Not the Gate," *Santa Cruz Sentinel*, 1:3.

344. "Honeymoon Couple," *Santa Cruz Evening News*, 8:4.

345. "Welch Arraigned," *Santa Cruz Evening News*, 8:3.

346. "English Picnic, Etc.," *Santa Cruz Sentinel*, 2.

347. "Big Tree Grove," *Santa Cruz Sentinel*, 4:3.

348. "The Felton Big Tree Grove," *Santa Cruz Sentinel*, 1:3.

349. "Hotel May Be Built," *Santa Cruz Sentinel*, 3:4.

350. "Interview with J. Welch," *Santa Cruz Morning Sentinel*, 3:4.

Chapter 16

351. Leonard, "An Hour with the Ince Movie Players," 6:4–5.

352. "Mayor Howe Says," *Santa Cruz Evening News*, 1:3–4.

353. Jessen, "In and Out of West Coast Studios," 845.

354. "Local and Personal," *North Platte Semi-Weekly Tribune*, 5:2.

355. Jessen, "In and Out of West Coast Studios," 4394.

356. "Hart Begins on His Film," *Santa Cruz Evening News*, 4:2.

357. Grace, "'Stunt Men,'" 33–34.

358. "Fox Has Most Original Picture Idea," *Moving Picture World*, 478.

Chapter 17

359. Jeter, "Welch Big Tree Grove," July 19, 1928, 2:3–4.

360. "Big Trees as State Park," *Santa Cruz Evening News*, 3:1.

361. No information has so far come to light on why, in 1928, the State of California did not select the grove for state park status.

362. "Santa Cruz Group Has 6 Months," *Santa Cruz Evening News*, 3:2.

363. Information obtained from Traci Bliss, great-grandniece of William Jeter.

364. Information provided by Lynn Stewart.

365. Information from Jim Kliment, April 2, 2019. Felton continued to have limited passenger rail service via Southern Pacific from Santa Cruz until 1965. Freight service ended in 1983.

366. "The Big Trees and the S.P.," *Riptide*, 1:3.

367. Nelson, "Stanley M. Hopkins."

368. In 1958, the Welch-era hotel buildings were damaged by fallen bay trees, and the California State Parks subsequently tore them down. It is uncertain when the old Cowell's Club House and cottages were removed, but photographic evidence shows them still standing in 1959.

BIBLIOGRAPHY

Address of President Roosevelt at Santa Cruz, California, May 11, 1903. Theodore Roosevelt Papers. Library of Congress Manuscript Division. Theodore Roosevelt Digital Library. Dickinson State University. www.theodorerooseveltcenter.org/Research/Digital-Library/Record?libID=o289816.

Arizona Republic. "Seaside and Mountain Santa Cruz a Resort." July 26, 1909, 12:1–2. Newspapers.com.

Armstrong, Edward Ambler. *The Sinaites: A Chronicle of Happy Days.* Princeton, NJ, 1922. Hathi Trust Digital Library, babel.hathitrust.org.

Aurora of the Valley [Newberry, VT]. "Lofty Trees." July 24, 1851, 1:4–5. Newspapers.com.

Barber, Edward. "Ingersoll's Cathedral." *The Conservator* 8, no. 10 (December 1897): 154. books.google.com.

Bartleson, John. "Oregon and California." *Wiskonsan Enquirer*, June 8, 1843, 1:5–6. Newspapers.com.

Beal, Chandra Moira, and Richard A. Beal. *Santa Cruz Beach Boardwalk: The Early Years: Never a Dull Moment.* N.p.: Pacific Group, n.d.

Beck, Warren A., and Ynez D. Hasse. "The Bear Flag Revolt and the Anglo-American Conquest of California." *Historical Atlas of California.* Norman: University of Oklahoma Press, 1975. www.militarymuseum.org.

Blakemore, Erin. "The Enslaved Native Americans Who Made the Gold Rush Possible." The History Channel, January 24, 2018. www.history.com.

Bliss, Traci, and Randall Brown. "Celebrity Visitors at Big Trees." In *Redwood Logging and Conservation in the Santa Cruz Mountains: A Split History*, 113. Santa Cruz, CA: Santa Cruz Museum of Art and History, 2014.

———. "Saving Big Basin: Heroes and Heroines." *In Redwood Logging and Conservation in the Santa Cruz Mountains: A Split History*, 117–28. Santa Cruz, CA: Santa Cruz Museum of Art and History, 2014.

———. "Which Welch?" *Redwood Logging and Conservation in the Santa Cruz Mountains: A Split History.* Santa Cruz, CA: Santa Cruz Museum of Art and History, 2014, 129.

Breckenridge, Thomas E. *Thomas E. Breckenridge Memoirs.* University of Missouri at Columbia: Western Historical Manuscripts Collection, 1894.

Brown, Randall, ed. *Trees with Names: Historical Walks through Henry Cowell State Park.* N.p.: 2008.

Brown, Randall, and Traci Bliss. "Two Trees for General Fremont." In *Redwood Logging and Conservation in the Santa Cruz Mountains: A Split History*, 100–12. Santa Cruz, CA: Santa Cruz Museum of Art and History, 2014.

"California Great Registers, 1866–1910." FamilySearch.org. Joseph Warren Welch, July 24, 1866; citing Voter Registration, 434 Fremont, San Francisco, California, United States, county clerk offices, California.

California Guide for Tourists and Settlers 1890. San Francisco: Carnall-Fitzhugh-Hopkins Company, 1890.

Casey, W.C. "End of the Line: Last Stagecoach to Santa Cruz." December 12, 2012. Patch.com.

Chase, J. Smeaton. *California Coast Trails: A Horseback Ride from Mexico to Oregon.* Boston: Houghton Mifflin Company, 1913.

Clarke, Chris. *Untold History: The Survival of California's Indians.* September 26, 2016. *Tending the Wild* series by KCET and the Autry Museum of the American West, 2019. www.kcet.org.

Clifford, Allen P. *From Geyser to Canon with Mary: Pilgrimage of Mary Commandery No. 36, Knights Templar of Pennsylvania to the Twenty-Ninth Triennial Conclave of the Grand Encampment U.S. at San Francisco, Cal.* Philadelphia: Thomson Printing Company, 1904. Internet Archive, archive.org.

Clinton, George W. "A California Giant to Be Dedicated." *San Francisco Call*, June 25, 1911, 35:7. Newspapers.com.

Colegrove, George L. *The Life Story of George L. Colegrove, Pioneer California Stage Driver and Railroad Man, as Told by Himself.* Oakland, CA, 1932. Repr., New York, 1974.

Cook, Lawrence F. *The Giant Sequoias of California.* Washington, D.C.: United States Government Printing Office, 1955. www.nps.gov.

Crawford, Michael J., ed. *The World Cruise of the Great White Fleet.* Washington D.C.: Naval Historical Center, Department of the Navy, 1908. Repr., 2008.

Curtis, William E. "Trees of Santa Cruz." *Evening Star* [Washington, D.C.], September 15, 1905, 12:2. Newspapers.com.

Cuthrell, Dr. Rob Q. "Quiroste Valley Cultural Preserve." Coastside State Parks Association, June 1, 2016, slide presentation. www.coastsidestateparks.org.

Daily Alta California. "Notes of a Trip of the S.F.B.D. Agricultural Society." August 27, 1860, 1:2. California Digital Newspaper Collection.

———. "The Railroad Picnic." June 9, 1889, 1:3. California Digital Newspaper Collection.

Daily Evening Herald [Stockton, CA]. "Fire in the Mountains Near Santa Cruz." July 10, 1867, 1:4. Newspapers.com.

The Daily Intelligencer [Seattle, WA]. "General Fremont." June 5, 1878, 1:2. Library of Congress Chronicling America.

Denton, Sally. "Frémont Steals California." *American Heritage* 60, no. 4 (Winter 2011): 1–5. www.americanheritage.com.

Deseret Evening News. "In the Midst of Tall Timber: President Wanders among the Santa Cruz Big Trees." May 12, 1903, 9:5. Newspapers.com.

Dunn, Robert Lee. "Roosevelt-Democrat." *Success Magazine* 10, no. 158 (July 1907): 463–66, 510–12. books.google.com.

Encyclopaedia Britannica. "James Jackson Jeffries: American Boxer." April 12, 2018. www.britannica.com.

Epting, Chris. *Teddy Roosevelt in California: The Whistle Stop Tour that Changed America.* Charleston, SC: The History Press, 2015.

Erk, Edmund Frederick. "A Merry Crusade to the Golden Gate, Allegheny Commandery, No. 35, Knights Templar, Allegheny, Pennsylvania, Twenty-Ninth Triennial Conclave, Grand Encampment." San Francisco: Knights Templar, September 1904.

Filmer, Ann. "Decoding the Redwoods: As Threats to California's Giant Redwoods Grow, Their Salvation Might Be in Their Complex Genetic Code." Department of Plant Sciences, College of Agricultural and Environmental Sciences, February 12, 2018. www.plantsciences.ucdavis.edu.

Fremont, John Charles. *Memoirs of My Life by John Charles Fremont. Including in the Narrative Five Journeys of Western Exploration, During the Years 1842, 1843–4, 1845–6–7, 1848–9, 1853–4. Together with a Sketch of the Life of Senator Benton, in Connection with Western Expansion by Jessie Benton Fremont. A Retrospect of Fifty Years Covering the Most Eventful Periods of Modern American History. With Maps and Colored Plates.* Vol. 1. Chicago: Belford, Clarke & Company, 1887, Hathi Trust Digital Library, babel.hathitrust.org.

Garvin, Martha Jane. *The Grizzly Bear* 9, no. 2, Native Sons of the Golden West (June 1911): 6. books.google.com.

———. "Trip to the Redwood in August with the Ice-man." *Overland Monthly* 56, no. 2 (1910): 301–7. books.google.com.

Goode, Barry. "A Pretty Obstinate Set of Fellows." In *Redwood Logging and Conservation in the Santa Cruz Mountains: A Split History.* Santa Cruz, CA: Santa Cruz Museum of Art and History, 2014, 31–40.

Gordon, Laura De Force. "Down the Coast." *Santa Cruz Weekly Sentinel*, September 29, 1877, 1:4. Newspapers.com.

Grace, Dick. "'Stunt Men': The Boys Who Risk Their Lives to Thrill." *Photoplay*, July–December 1925, 33–34. archive.org.

Greene, J.W. "The Big Trees of California." *The Western Fruit-Grower* 15, no. 8 (August 1904): 270. books.google.com.

Griswold, N.W. *Beauties of California: Including Big Trees, Yosemite Valley, Geysers, Lake Tahoe, Donner Lake, S.F. '49 & '83, etc.* San Francisco: H.S. Crocker & Company, 1883. Hathi Trust Digital Library, babel.hathitrust.org.

Hamilton, E.H. "Santa Cruz Had More Tact than San Jose." *Santa Cruz Morning Sentinel*, May 13, 1903, 1:5. Newspapers.com.

Hamman, Rick. *California Central Coast Railways.* Boulder, CO: Pruett Publishing Company, 1980.

Hardy, Lady Duffus. *Through Cities and Prairie Lands: Sketches of an American Tour.* Chicago: Belford, Clarke, and Company, 1882.

Harrison, Edward Sanford. *History of Santa Cruz County, California.* San Francisco: Pacific Press Publishing Company, 1892, 532. Hathi Trust Digital Library, babel.hathitrust.org.

Heath, Kate. "At a Watering Place." *Sacramento Daily Union*, July 13, 1878, 2:5–6. Newspapers.com.

Hoitt, Ira G. *Pacific Coast Guide and Programme of the Knights Templar Triennial Conclave at San Francisco, August 1883.* San Francisco: Triennial Committee, 1883.

Holder, C.F. "How a Forest Fire Was Extinguished with Wine." *Wide World Magazine* 5, no. 28 (August 1900): 338–48. archive.org.

Howard, Winifred. *Howard of Glossop's Journal of a Tour: In the United States, Canada and Mexico.* London: Sampson Low, Marston and Company, Limited, 1897.

Huxsaw, A. "California Big Trees Visited." *Mahoning Dispatch* [Canfield, OH], June 30, 1916, 8:3–4. Newspapers.com.

Hylkema, Mark G. "The Native American Cultural Landscape of the Santa Cruz Mountains and Northern Monterey Bay Coast." In *Redwood Logging and Conservation in the Santa Cruz Mountains: A Split History*, edited by Lisa Robinson, 15–25. Santa Cruz, CA: Santa Cruz Museum of Art and History, 2014.

Impulse. "The Carnegies Visit Santa Cruz." 48, December 2016. www.carnegiehero.org.

Jepson, Willis Linn. *Jepson Field Book*, August 18, 1910, 180. Jepson Herbaria Archives, University of California–Berkeley. ucjeps.berkeley.edu.

Jessen, J.C. "Hart Feature Renamed." *Motion Picture News* 16, no. 25, December 22, 1917, 4394. archive.org.

———. "In and Out of West Coast Studios." *Motion Picture News*, January–February 1916, 844. archive.org.

Jeter, William T. "The Welch Big Tree Grove." *Santa Cruz Evening News*, July 18, 1928, 3:2–4. Newspapers.com.

———. "The Welch Big Tree Grove." *Santa Cruz Evening News*, July 19, 1928, 2:3–4. Newspapers.com.

Koch, John Felix, and George Wharton. *California: Our Western Wonderland*. Chicago: A. Flanagan Company, 1927.

Koch, Margaret. "He Sailed into Town 50 Years Ago." *Santa Cruz Sentinel*, August 24, 1969, 22:1–3. Newspapers.com.

———. "Talley-ho Trip to Our Redwood Groves Left Visitors Speechless." *Santa Cruz Sentinel*, March 28, 1965, 8:1. Newspapers.com.

Leek, E.B. "Our California Letter." *Sag-Harbor Express*, May 15, 1902, 1:7. New York State Historic Newspapers, nyshistoricnewspapers.org.

Leonard, James P. "An Hour with the Ince Movie Players in the Santa Cruz Mountains." *Santa Cruz Evening News*, December 22, 1915, 6:4–5. Newspapers.com.

Lewis, Bill. "John C. Fremont and the Klamath Basin." *Klamath County Historical Society Trumpeter* 112 (Fall 2018). klamathcountyhistoricalsociety.org.

Lexington [MO] Intelligencer. "A Missourian's View of the 'Golden West' and the Route He Took to Reach It." December 25, 1886, 1:6–7. Newspapers.com.

Los Angeles Herald. "Fremont Coming Home." May 5, 1888, 1:6. Newspapers.com.

MacDougall, Laurie. "Henry Cowell and His Family (1819–1955)." S.H. Cowell Foundation, Santa Cruz Public Libraries Local History. history.santacruzpl.org.

MacFadden, Harry Alexander. *Rambles in the Far West*. Holidaysburg, PA: Standard Printing House, 1906. Hathi Trust Digital Library, babel.hathitrust.org.

Manna, Salvatore, and Shannon Dixon Van Zant. *Brands of Calaveras County, California 1854–1880*. N.p.: CreateSpace Independent Publishing Platform, January 15, 2017.

Masters, Ryan. "The Horrors of the Summit Tunnel." December 8, 2014. Hilltromper.com.

McCrackin, Josephine Clifford. "Carnegie Entertained." *Santa Cruz Sentinel*, March 12, 1910, 2:5. Newspapers.com.

———. "'New' Santa Cruz and the Big Trees." *Santa Cruz Sentinel*, August 16, 1903, 4:1. Newspapers.com.

McKinley, Mike. "Cruise of the Great White Fleet." September 5, 2017. Navy History and Heritage Command. www.history.navy.mil.

McPherson, Duncan. "An Artistic Souvenir." *Santa Cruz Sentinel*, May 14, 1901, 2:1. Newspapers.com.

———. "The Big Tree Outrage." *Santa Cruz Sentinel*, July 17, 1897, 2:1. Newspapers.com.

The Midland Journal [Rising Sun, MD]. "Under the Big Redwood Trees." May 8, 1908, 2. Library of Congress, Chronicling America.

Miles, Jake. "Santa Cruz: Her Mammoth Trees." *Utah Enquirer*, August 21, 1888, 1:7. Utah Digital Newspapers.

M'Isaac, Colin H. "Invitation to President Taft." *Santa Cruz Sentinel*, July 15, 1909, 5:5. Newspapers.com.

Mountain Echo. "The President's Visit." May 16, 1903, 2:1–4.

Moving Picture World. "Fox Has Most Original Picture Idea in 'The Last Man on Earth.'" July–August 1924, 478. archive.org.

Muir, John. Letter to Jeanne C. Carr, September 3, 1877. John Muir Correspondence, University of the Pacific Library, Holt-Atherton Special Collections.

Nash, Roderick. *Wilderness and the American Mind*. Rev. ed. New Haven, CT: Yale University Press, 1973.

National Park Service. "Historic Resources of Big Basin Redwoods State Park." National Register of Historic Places Program. National Register of Historic Places Multiple Property Documentation Form. www.nps.gov.

———. "Redwood Burl." Redwood National and State Parks bulletin, n.d. www. nps.gov.

Nelson, Robert L. "Stanley M. Hopkins (1944/8/25)." Remembering Our Own: The Santa Cruz County Military Roll of Honor 1861–2010. Santa Cruz Museum of Art and History, 2010. history.santacruzpl.org.

North Platte [NE] Semi-Weekly Tribune. "Local and Personal." August 24, 1917, 5:2. Newspapers.com.

Nye, Edgar W. "Under the Big Trees." *Seattle Post-Intelligencer*, April 30, 1893, 14:3. Newspapers.com.

Ohlenkamp, H. "Tells of Choir's Excursion to the Coast." *Ogden Standard*, April 2, 1903, 5:4. Newspapers.com.

Orleans County Monitor [Barton, VT]. "California in Retrospect." January 16, 1899, 1:3. Newspapers.com.

Otto, Ernest. "Old Santa Cruz by Ernest Otto." *Santa Cruz Sentinel*, August 15, 1948, 11:7. Newspapers.com.

Pacific Sentinel. "Sayante Valley: Fremont's Tree." June 28, 1856, 2:4. California Digital Newspaper Collection.

Palmquist, Peter E., and Thomas R. Kailbourn. *Pioneer Photographers of the Far West: A Biographical Dictionary, 1840–1865*. Palo Alto, CA: Stanford University Press, 2000. books.google.com.

Patten, Phyllis. "Loss of Historical Aspects of Henry Cowell Park Is Mourned." *Santa Cruz Sentinel*, January 11, 1959, 18:5–8. Newspapers.com.

Perry, Frank. "Dissecting 'Jumbo': A Picture Postcard History." Santa Cruz Museum of Art and History, January 5, 2015, 1. Online History Journal of Santa Cruz County, santacruzmah.imgix.net.

———. "Who Was Henry Cowell?" Friends of the Cowell Lime Works, University of California–Santa Cruz. October 10, 2015. limeworks.ucsc.edu.

Perry, Frank A., Robert W. Piwarzyk, Michael D. Luther, Alverda Orlando, Allan Molho and Sierra L. Perry. *Lime Kiln Legacies: The History of the Lime Industry in Santa Cruz County*. Santa Cruz, CA: Museum of Art and History at the McPherson Center, 2007.

Phillips, Morris. *Abroad and at Home: Practical Hints for Tourists.* New York: Brentano's, 1891. archive.org.

Phillips, Tom. "Town of Mariposa: A Short History." Mariposa Museum and History Center, 2018. mariposamuseum.com.

Piwarzyk, Robert W., and Michael L. Miller. *Valley of Redwoods: A Guide to Henry Cowell Redwoods State Park.* Felton, CA: Mountain Parks Foundation, 2006.

Porter, Albert J. "Naval History Made as Santa Cruz Dedicates Giant Redwood to Rodman, Fleet and Personnel." *San Francisco Chronicle*, August 27, 1919, 1:1. Newspapers.com.

Price, Arthur. "Fifteen Hundred Bluejackets Are Piloted Through the Big Trees by Fair Guides." *San Francisco Call*, May 4, 1908, 2:2. Newspapers.com.

Raymond, Isabel Hammel. *Santa Cruz County: Resources, Advantages, Objects of Interest.* Santa Cruz Development Association, 1887. www.loc.gov/item/rc01000611.

Reader, Phil. "To Know My Name: A Chronological History of African Americans in Santa Cruz County." history.santacruzpl.org.

Remarks of President Roosevelt at the Big Tree Grove, Santa Cruz, California, May 11, 1903. Theodore Roosevelt Papers. Library of Congress Manuscript Division. www.theodorerooseveltcenter.org.

Rideout, Mrs. J.B. *Camping Out in California.* San Francisco: R.R. Patterson, 1889, 175–77. www.loc.gov/item/rc01000881.

Rizzo, Martin. "Indigenous Justice or Padre Killers? Lino, Fausta, & the Assassination of Padre Quintana." In *Do You Know My Name?*, 12. Santa Cruz, CA: Santa Cruz Museum of Art and History, 2016.

Robinson, Lisa. "Hopkins' Big Trees." *Santa Cruz Mountain Bulletin* 5, no. 11 (November–December 2016).

———. *The San Lorenzo Valley.* Images of America. Charleston, SC: Arcadia Publishing, 2012.

———. "The San Lorenzo Valley Flume Chronicle." In *Redwood Logging and Conservation in the Santa Cruz Mountains: A Split History*, 51–59. Santa Cruz, CA: Santa Cruz Museum of Art and History, 2014.

Roosevelt, Theodore. "Remarks at the Big Tree Grove in Santa Cruz, California." Felton, California, May 11, 1903. www.presidency.ucsb.edu.

Ryland, Judge. "A Missourian's Letter." *Santa Cruz Sentinel*, January 9, 1887, 2:1. Newspapers.com.

Sacramento Daily Union. "Pacific Coast Items." November 15, 1875, 1:3. California Digital Newspaper Collection.

———. "Sayante Valley: Fremont's Tree." July 3, 1856, 2:4. California Digital Newspaper Collection.

San Francisco Call. "Charity Does Harm Thinks Skibo's Laird." March 12, 1910, 10:3. Newspapers.com.

———. "Dance Under the Big Trees." June 30, 1896, 4:5. Newspapers.com.

———. "Memorial Gift from Nebraska." June 4, 1904, 3:6. Newspapers.com.

———. "Undefeated Champion Will Have a Tree Named for Him." April 8, 1910, 10:2. Newspapers.com.

———. "You Are Immense, Is Captain's Vote." May 5, 1908, 5:2. Newspapers.com.

San Francisco Chronicle. "Cowell Dies and Assailant in Jail." August 5, 1903, 12:5. Newspapers.com.

———. "Hopkins' Big Tree Grove." May 15, 1910, 34:5. Newspapers.com.

———. "Santa Cruz Big Trees: Peculiarities of Their Growth." June 9, 1889, 2:5. Newspapers.com.

———. "Santa Cruz Entertains the Cabinet Royally." May 14, 1901, 3:1–4. Newspapers.com.

———. "Santa Cruz Jubilant." October 15, 1875, 3:3. Newspapers.com.

San Francisco Examiner. "The Pathfinder: General Fremont Revisits the Big Trees, Which He Saw 46 Years Ago." May 11, 1888, 4:7. Newspapers.com.

Santa Cruz County Times. "Notes of a Trip to the Zayante." August 1, 1868, 2:2–3.

Santa Cruz Courier. "The Santa Cruz Big Trees." April 26, 1877.

Santa Cruz Daily Sentinel. "The Big Trees: Endeavorers Will Be Admitted to the Grove Free of Charge." July 17, 1897, 1:2. Newspapers.com.

Santa Cruz Daily Surf. "At the Big Trees—Reception to Gen. Fremont." May 5, 1888, 4:5.

———. "The Big Trees." June 8, 1889, 2:1–2.

———. "The Big Trees." October 9, 1884, 2:2.

———. "Felton and Ben Lomond." March 26, 1891, 1:2.

———. "Greeting—How Santa Cruz Will Welcome the President." May 1, 1891, 3:5.

———. "The Latest Camp," June 16, 1883, 3:4.

———. "Picked Up on Pacific Avenue." February 16, 1901, 1:1.

———. "The President's Day in Santa Cruz." May 13, 1903, 1:1–6.

———. "The President with a Party of Distinguished Guests Honored and Welcomed in Santa Cruz, the City of the Holy Cross." May 2, 1891, 3–5.

———. "The Railroad Picnic: The Largest and Finest Excursion Picnic Ever Held in This County." June 10, 1889, 3:5.

———. "We Did Our Best." May 13, 1901, 1:1–5.

Santa Cruz Evening News. "Big Trees as State Park." March 6, 1928, 3:1. Newspapers.com.

———. "The Big Trees for the People." April 30, 1908, 2:3. Newspapers.com.

———. "Big Trees Guide Is Dead, Age 65." October 28, 1929, 2:1. Newspapers.com.

———. "Burned in Effigy at Big Tree Grove." May 19, 1910, 1:6–7. Newspapers.com.

———. "Forest Giant Bears Tablet Commemorating Pacific Fleet." June 29, 1921, 4:2. Newspapers.com.

———. "Hart Begins on His Film of Days of Gold." March 15, 1920, 4:2. Newspapers.com.

———. "Henry Staley, Famed Guide, Dies at 68." March 18, 1941, 1:3. Newspapers.com.

———. "Honeymoon Couple from Reno Figure in Lively Incident at Big Trees." October 22, 1918, 8:4. Newspapers.com.

———. "Inside and Outside by Brent." April 14, 1932, 1:1. Newspapers.com.

———. "Locates Redwood Burl Stumpage for Curios." February 8, 1921, 6:3. Newspapers.com.

———. "Mayor Howe Says Movie Men Must Get Santa Cruz Habit: Tells of His Trip." January 4, 1916, 1:3–4. Newspapers.com.

———. "Santa Cruz Group Has 6 Months to Dispose of Historic Welch Ranch." August 1, 1927, 1:7 and 3:2.

———. "Sing, O, Redwoods." April 9, 1910, 3:1–2. Newspapers.com.

———. "Up Among the Big Trees." August 15, 1911, 2:2.

———. "Welch Arraigned on Battery Charge." October 23, 1918, 8:3. Newspapers.com.

———. "Your Vacation Is Not Complete Without a Visit to the Famous Big Trees." August 4, 1916, 7:5. Newspapers.com.

Santa Cruz Evening Sentinel. April 24, 1900, 3:1. Newspapers.com.

———. March 28, 1901, 2:2. Newspapers.com.

———. May 30, 1902, 3:1. Newspapers.com.

———. "Santa Cruz Big Trees Said to Be in Danger." March 13, 1900, 4:3. Newspapers.com.

Santa Cruz Morning Sentinel. "Interview with J. Welch Regarding the Big Trees." July 8, 1902, 3:4. Newspapers.com.

———. "Passing Away of Mrs. Welch." January 10, 1905, 1:2. Newspapers.com.

———. "Santa Cruz Big Trees Said to Be in Danger." March 13, 1900, 4:3. Newspapers.com.

Santa Cruz Sentinel. "Annual High Jinks." September 8, 1885, 3:3. Newspapers.com.

———. "At Headquarters—Notes and Decorations for Admission Day." September 9, 1888, 3:3. Newspapers.com.

———. August 5, 1893, 3:3. Newspapers.com.

———. August 13, 1891, 2:1. Newspapers.com.

———. "Axmen Spared Not the Gate." August 15, 1911, 1:3. Newspapers.com.

———. "The Bangos: Ladies' Day among the Boys at the Big Trees." September 11, 1885, 3:6. Newspapers.com.

———. "A Big Man among the Big Trees." March 12, 1910, 1:5. Newspapers.com.

———. "Big Tree Grove—Firms in This City Are Negotiating with Owners for Purchase of Great Forest." July 2, 1902, 4:3. Newspapers.com.

———. "Big Tree Grove Hotel." July 8, 1885, 4:4. Newspapers.com.

———. "Big Trees Guide Is Critically Ill." March 18, 1941, 1:5. Newspapers.com.

———. "The Busch Party." March 21, 1886, 4:4. Newspapers.com.

———. "A Delighted Artist—Thos. Nast Enthuses Over Santa Cruz." May 5, 1888, 3:4. Newspapers.com.

———. "Died Suddenly." March 12, 1901, 3:1. Newspapers.com.

———. "English Picnic, Etc." August 10, 1902, 2:3. Newspapers.com.

———. February 23, 1897, 2:2. Newspapers.com.

———. "Felton: A Village in the Mountains of Santa Cruz County." March 31, 1887, 3:3. Newspapers.com.

———. "The Felton Big Tree Grove." August 20, 1902, 1:3. Newspapers.com.

———. "Felton Items." July 7, 1885, 2:4. Newspapers.com.

———. "Felton Items." June 9, 1885, 2:3. Newspapers.com.

———. "Fremont Reception." May 5, 1888, 3:2. Newspapers.com.

———. "Gustav Rohrer, Known Here, Dies." August 13, 1941, 8:1. Newspapers.com.

———. "A Hotel May Be Built at Big Trees." June 13, 1902, 3:4. Newspapers.com.

———. "Jos. Ball's Statement." March 28, 1891, 3:3. Newspapers.com.

———. July 29, 1902, 2:4. Newspapers.com.

———. June 1, 1892, 3:1. Newspapers.com.

———. June 23, 1886, 3:3. Newspapers.com.

———. June 25, 1889, 3:1. Newspapers.com.

———. "Local News." August 3, 1904, 3:1. Newspapers.com.

———. "Local News." January 25, 1905, 3:2. Newspapers.com.

———. March 10, 1900, 2:4. Newspapers.com.

———. March 13, 1900, 3:2. Newspapers.com.

———. March 28, 1891, 3:2. Newspapers.com.

———. May 2, 1891, 2:1. Newspapers.com.

———. May 5, 1891, 3:2. Newspapers.com.

———. May 7, 1886, 3:2. Newspapers.com.

———. "M.C. Hopkins' Narrow Escape." April 21, 1906, 3:2. Newspapers.com.

———. "Millionaire Cowell: Town Talk." March 13, 1903, 4:1. Newspapers.com.

———. "Miscellaneous." May 29, 1902, 3:3. Newspapers.com.

———. October 1, 1884, 3:1. Newspapers.com.

———. "A Pleasure Trip—How Adolphus Busch Is Celebrating His Silver Wedding Anniversary." March 20, 1886, 5:5. Newspapers.com.

———. "The Railroad Picnic." June 9, 1889, 3:5. Newspapers.com.

———. "San Lorenzo Valley Items." July 29, 1902, 3:4. Newspapers.com.

———. "Santa Cruz." April 23, 1891, 1:4. Newspapers.com.

———. "Santa Cruz Big Trees." April 1, 1902. Newspapers.com.

———. "Santa Cruz Yesterdays." August 8, 1948, 4:4–7. Newspapers.com.

———. September 17, 1907, 10:5. Newspapers.com.

———. "Social and Personal." March 5, 1897, 3:3. Newspapers.com.

———. "A Tough Crowd." May 20, 1890, 1:7. Newspapers.com.

———. "A Trip to Felton." June 29, 1884, 1:6. Newspapers.com.

———. "The Visit of President Roosevelt." May 12, 1903, 1:3–6. Newspapers.com.

Santa Cruz Weekly Sentinel. "At the Big Trees." May 7, 1881, 2:2. Newspapers.com.

———. August 18, 1877, 2:9. Newspapers.com.

———. "Curiosities of Santa Cruz." November 8, 1862, 2:3. Newspapers.com.

———. "Death of a Pioneer." May 30, 1868, 2:1. Newspapers.com.

———. "Episcopal Church Picnic." August 17, 1878, 3:5. Newspapers.com.

———. "Felton Items." June 28, 1879, 3:6. Newspapers.com.

———. "Felton Items." September 23, 1876, 3:3. Newspapers.com.

———. "Felton Letter." June 12, 1880, 2:3. Newspapers.com.

———. "Fremont's Saplings." June 13, 1874, 3:2. Newspapers.com.

———. "A Gala Day." October 16, 1875, 3:4. Newspapers.com.

———. "Hawaiian Singers Make Great Hit." June 17, 1905, 3:4. Newspapers.com.

———. July 29, 1882, 2:4. Newspapers.com.

———. "Mammoth Trees." July 2, 1870, 2:3. Newspapers.com.

———. May 4, 1878, 3:3. Newspapers.com.

———. May 12, 1877, 3:3. Newspapers.com.

———. May 19, 1877, 2:5. Newspapers.com.

———. May 26, 1877, 3:2. Newspapers.com.

———. May 27, 1882, 2:1. Newspapers.com.

———. November 20, 1875, 3:1. Newspapers.com.

———. October 8, 1881, 3:4. Newspapers.com.

———. "Real Estate Transactions." January 4, 1868, 2:4. Newspapers.com.

———. "Santa Cruz Letter." July 12, 1879, 2:2–3. Newspapers.com.

———. "A Selfish Policy." May 4, 1878, 2:1. Newspapers.com.

———. "The South Pacific Coast Railroad." August 24, 1878, 2:3. Newspapers.com.

———. "S.P.C.R.R." April 22, 1882, 3:5–6. Newspapers.com.

———. "Summer Recreation in the Open Air." January 15, 1876, 3:2. Newspapers.com.

———. "Visit of a Renowned Botanist." August 3, 1872, 2:3. Newspapers.com.

———. "What They Saw." October 23, 1875, 3:4. Newspapers.com.

———. "Workingmen's Picnic." September 14, 1878, 3:5–6. Newspapers.com.

Six and a Half Tenderfeet: Toward the Sunrise on "The Sunset." The Record of a Journey in the Land of Sunshine. New York: World's Work Press, 1903, 10–11. Hathi Trust Digital Library, babel.hathitrust.org.

South Pacific Coast Railroad advertisement, date unknown.

State of California. *Appendix to the Journals of the Senate and Assembly of the Twenty-Seventh Session of the Legislature of the State of California.* Vol. 7. Sacramento, CA: State Printing Office, 1887, 283. books.google.com.

Taylor, Arthur A. "Santa Cruz by the Sea." *Sunset Magazine* 10, no. 1 (November 1902): 419–33.

The Tennessean. "Big Trees—An Attraction." January 2, 1903, 2:4. Newspapers.com.

Tweed, William. *King Sequoia: The Tree that Inspired a Nation, Created Our National Park System, and Changed the Way We Think about Nature.* Berkeley, CA: Heyday Books, 2016.

Vandervort, Mrs. W.E. "California Epistle." *Herald-Advance* [Milbank, SD], June 26, 1908, 1:6. Library of Congress Chronicling America.

Vermont Phœnix [Brattleboro, VT]. "A House in California One Thousand Years Old." March 28, 1873, 4:3. Newspapers.com.

Vessey, Professor C.E. "Economy of the Vegetable Kingdom." *Pacific Rural Press*, March 6, 1875, 9:1. California Digital Newspaper Collection.

Vischer, Edward. *Vischer's Pictorial of California Landscape, Trees, and Forest Scenes: Grand Features of California Scenery, Life, Traffic, and Customs.* San Francisco: Joseph Winterburn and Company, April 1870. books.google.com.

Westfield [NY] Republican. "California—Monterey, Santa Cruz, and the Big Trees." July 18, 1883, 2:4. nyshistoricnewspapers.org.

Whaley, Derek. "Railroads: Roaring Camp & Big Trees Narrow Gauge Railroad." Santa Cruz Trains: Railroads of the Monterey Bay Area, 2012–18. www.santacruztrains.com.

———. *Santa Cruz Trains: Railroads of the Santa Cruz Mountains.* N.p.: CreateSpace Independent Publishing Platform, 2015.

"What Is a Name: The Golden Gate?" The Golden Gate Bridge Highway and Transportation District, 2006–18. goldengatebridge.org.

Willey, S.H. *Santa Cruz County, California: Illustrations Descriptive of Its Scenery, Fine Residences, Public Buildings, Manufactories, Hotels, Farm Scenes, Business Houses, Schools, Churches, Mines, Mills, Etc.…With Historical Sketch of the County.* San Francisco: Wallace W. Elliott and Company, 1879. Hathi Trust Digital Library, babel. hathitrust.org.

Wilson, Scott. "Decoding the Redwoods." *Washington Post*, February 7, 2018. www.washingtonpost.com.

Worth, Zitella. *59 of '86 Letters Written to the Lebanon Courier During the Summer of 1886.* Lebanon, PA: Reinoehl Publishing, 1886. books.google.com.

INDEX

Wintu 27
Workingmen's Club 62
World War II 150
Wrights 60, 181

Y

Yana 27
Yellowstone 37, 45, 140
YMCA Tree 70, 71
Yokut 17
Yosemite 37, 40, 73, 118, 123
  Yosemite Grant Act 118
  Yosemite National Park 118
  Yosemite wagon 40
Young Men's Christian Association 70,
    71

Z

Zayante Creek 15, 19, 20, 24, 35, 64
Zayante settlement 20, 24, 26, 171

ABOUT THE AUTHOR

Deborah Osterberg volunteers at Henry Cowell Redwoods State Park, where, in period dress, she interprets the resort-era history of Big Trees Grove. While obtaining a degree in history and geography at California State University– Chico, Deborah worked seasonally for the National Park Service (NPS) starting at Yellowstone National Park. After graduate study at the University of California– Santa Barbara, she returned to Sequoia National Park, where she began a career in curation and helped arrange centennial commemorations for California's first national park. Later, Deborah served as the lead interpreter at Eugene O'Neill National Historic Site in Danville, California. She became a Civil War abolitionist reenactor while serving as museum curator of Fort Sumter National Monument in Charleston, South Carolina. She also managed museum collections of Charles Pinckney National Historic Site and Moores Creek National Battlefield. At Mount Rainier National Park in 1999, Deborah assisted with another park centennial celebration and helped establish the park archives. For ten years she worked at the National Archives at San Francisco, specializing in Bureau of Indian Affairs records. Deborah now lives in Bonny Doon.